The information in *We Promise* has been an indispensable resource for engaged and married couples alike in our church. The wisdom that comes from years of marriage combined with clinical expertise and Holy Spirit anointing upon Dan and Penny makes this manual a rare treasure. I highly recommend this for anyone who is interested in building marriages that stand the tests of time."

—Lee Cummings, Sr. Pastor, Radiant Church

We Promise is without a doubt today's best tool for marriage preparation. Penny and Dan have thought this syllabus through down to the smallest detail. In addition to the vision Penny received from God, their years of teaching pre-marriage couples as well as their counseling of married couples have given them a sensitive and loving approach to the relational issues of marriage.

This manual workbook is a must for all married couples and those looking forward to marriage. It will also be one of those manuals couples will want to review periodically; sort of a "Let's see how we are doing" checkup. Today's pastors will enjoy using this tool in their pre-marriage counseling.

—Reverend Dr. Bill Greenfield, Ph.D.
Hospital Care Pastor, Radiant Church

We Promise recognizes that a God-honoring, joy-filled marriage does not happen. It requires devotion and hard work. Christian couples who refuse to settle for mediocrity will find here a most helpful marriage building tool."

—Reverend Mark Minegar
Associate Pastor, Hillcrest Christian Reformed Church

Most marriages in America are in serious trouble, with the divorce rate climbing higher and higher. Thus, I am always looking for good books and seminars on this subject to recommend to counselees, who wish to better their relationships. *We Promise* is one of the best I've seen in a long time. Biblical principles are presented in a simplistic, practical manner; offering hope, joy and peace, which is so lacking in our society today. I recommend this book highly to all couples, regardless of age or past troubles; and I, also, recommend Dr. Dan and Penny Loosenort to hold seminars in churches and Christian ministries.

—Reverend Dr. Ben Fulayter
Senior Pastor, Clayton Bible Church

We Promise explains in detail what "The Promise" is that you are about to take as a soon-to-be married couple. It is worth your time to study the manual and answer the questions with one another. Do not rush through this manual. Anything worth doing is worth doing well. Communication is the key to avoiding the pitfalls of life, especially married life. As I think back to the thousands of people who came through the Healing Rooms of Grand Rapids with baggage in their marriage, this manual would have saved them from their many burdens. Most Christians today have lots of baggage when we are supposed to have luggage. Baggage pulls you down as you drag it around. Luggage is something you pack for a purposeful trip and destination. *We Promise* is a must for your luggage!

—Reverend Mark L. Gurley, CLU, ChFC
Co-founder of the Healing Rooms of Grand Rapids
Founder of the Supernatural Training Center
Financial advisor since 1988

We promise

18 Foundational Stones for
an Unshakeable Marriage

PENNY LOOSENORT
Rev. Dr. Daniel Loosenort

Tate Publishing & Enterprises

We Promise
Copyright © 2011 by Penny and Rev. Dr. Daniel Loosenort. All rights reserved.

No part of this publication may be reproduced, stored in a retrieval system or transmitted in any way by any means, electronic, mechanical, photocopy, recording or otherwise without the prior permission of the author except as provided by USA copyright law.

Scripture quotations marked (NKJV) are taken from the New King James Version®. Copyright © 1982 by Thomas Nelson, Inc. Used by permission. All rights reserved.

Scripture quotations marked (ESV) are from The Holy Bible, English Standard Version®, copyright © 2001 by Crossway Bibles, a publishing ministry of Good News Publishers. Used by permission. All rights reserved.

Scripture quotations marked "NIV" are taken from the *Holy Bible, New International Version* ®, Copyright © 1973, 1978, 1984 by International Bible Society. Used by permission of Zondervan Publishing House. All rights reserved.

Scripture quotations marked "MSG" are taken from *The Message*, Copyright © 1993, 1994, 1995, 1996, 2000, 2001, 2002. Used by permission of NavPress Publishing Group. All rights reserved.

Hebrew definitions: Hebrew Strong's Concordance

Italics were added to some scriptures for added emphasis

This book is designed to provide accurate and authoritative information with regard to the subject matter covered. This information is given with the understanding that neither the author nor Tate Publishing, LLC is engaged in rendering legal, professional advice. Since the details of your situation are fact dependent, you should additionally seek the services of a competent professional.

The opinions expressed by the author are not necessarily those of Tate Publishing, LLC.

Published by Tate Publishing & Enterprises, LLC
127 E. Trade Center Terrace | Mustang, Oklahoma 73064 USA
1.888.361.9473 | www.tatepublishing.com

Tate Publishing is committed to excellence in the publishing industry. The company reflects the philosophy established by the founders, based on Psalm 68:11,
"The Lord gave the word and great was the company of those who published it."

Book design copyright © 2011 by Tate Publishing, LLC. All rights reserved.
Cover design by Kristen Verser
Interior design by Joel Uber

Published in the United States of America

ISBN: 978-1-61777-777-6
1. Religion: Christian Life, Love & Marriage
2. Religion: Christian Education, General
11.05.26

Dedication

We dedicate this manual to our daughters. We are so proud of each of you, what you have accomplished so far, and the great plans the Lord has for each of you that are yet to be fulfilled. As your parents, we are truly blessed to have been able to watch each of you grow, mature, marry, and raise children of your own. We truly wish we had known what we do now when we were raising you girls. May your marriages truly be radiant and have the fragrant aroma of Christ Jesus upon them. May the richness of the abundance of God always chase you down and overtake you. May our grandchildren flourish in the courts of our God.

We love you all!

Dad and Mom

Acknowledgments

First and foremost, we must give glory and praise to the King of kings, the Lord of lords, the Great Almighty, our Father, Savior, and King. No words could ever express how grateful we are to be in the kingdom of God.

We are extremely grateful to the following people for the time they spent proofreading this manual in order to bring it to perfection. Thank you: Danielle (our daughter) for the hours she spent proofreading and editing this manual. Danielle was truly a source of encouragement and insight into the world of writing. Jean Loosenort, Laverne Freeman, Dr. Bill and Mary Greenfield, Reverend Dr. Ben Fulayter, Mark and Michele Gurley, Barbara VanLoozenoord, and Jeff Blamer. A very special thank you to Dave and Patty Riegal for your prayer, support, encouragement, and belief that *We Promise* will change marriages.

Several years ago Pastor Lee Cummings asked us to oversee the pre-marriage couples at Radiant Church. We were humbled and considered it a privilege to take on such a task. *We Promise* may never have been written had it not been for this request and us responding to the call. Dan and I would like to thank Pastor Lee Cummings for entrusting us with the implementation and responsibility of overseeing the *Marital Foundations* program. *We Promise* is the reflection of several years of serving and counseling pre-marriage as well as married couples. We are thrilled to be part of a church that strives to put in place an unshakeable foundation for marriage.

Table of Contents

13	Foreword
15	Note from the Authors
17	Write Down the Revelation
21	We Believe Marriage Is
28	*Foundational Stone One*
29	Our Doctrinal Statement of Faith
39	*Foundational Stone Two*
41	I Now Pronounce You Husband and Wife
45	*The Role of the Husband*
54	*Foundational Stone Three*
55	*The Role of the Wife*
71	*Foundational Stone Four*
73	Honor Guards
88	*Foundational Stone Five*
89	*Foundational Stone Six*
90	*Foundational Stone Seven*
91	Ours for the Keeping: Sex and Intimacy
113	*Foundational Stone Eight*
114	*Foundational Stone Nine*

115	*Foundational Stone Ten*
117	The Torch of Tradition
124	*Foundational Stone Eleven*
125	Clashing Cymbals
141	*Conflict Resolution*
146	*Foundational Stone Twelve*
147	*Foundational Stone Thirteen*
148	*Foundational Stone Fourteen*
149	The Piggy Bank
156	*Preparing a Budget*
159	*Foundational Stone Fifteen*
161	A Loyal Heart and a Willing Mind
161	*Deepening Our Spiritual Walk*
170	*Raising Our Children in the Lord*
173	*Foundational Stone Sixteen*
174	*Foundational Stone Seventeen*
175	*Foundational Stone Eighteen*
177	Conclusion
179	Note to Leaders
181	Recommended Resources
183	End Notes

Foreword

We Promise will transform every marriage that desires to have Jesus Christ as the headship of their marriage. Reverend Dr. Daniel and Penny Loosenort have been led by the Holy Spirit to compile the scriptural references that guide us in many issues that affect our marriages. Never before have I seen a manual that illustrates so effectively the spoken Word of God and how to apply it in real life. *We Promise* is a blessing for every marriage! In the end, the Lord and all of heaven would rejoice, since all our Savior wants for us is peace, love, happiness, and to give to us the desires of our hearts! May the marriages this manual transforms be the beginning of the Lord's army to save our country that seems lost!

In Christian Service,
Reverend Steven M. Baran, D.D.
President/CEO
National Christian Counselors Association

Note from the Authors

On April 29, 1978, at one p.m., in Townsend Park, we made a promise to one another. Little did we know this promise would endure through over thirty years of marriage. With little preparation and lack of knowledge, we embarked on this journey. Trial and error were our teachers and companions for many years. We are forever grateful to our Lord who put an undying desire to press through and keep on keeping on! Our desire is that young couples embarking on marriage or those already in the trenches build a foundation upon which their house of marriage is unshakeable. Our desire is for marriages to truly be a reflection of the relationship of Jesus Christ and His bride!

In honor of marriage,
Dan and Penny

Write Down the Revelation

"Yes, Lord, I get it…I'll write it down in the morning when I get up." I'm very thankful the Lord continued to nudge me until I got up and wrote down what He was revealing to me. Normally when I dream, once morning has come and I wake up, very few details of that dream can be remembered. While I was dreaming, a promise was being written out for me in the dream: single sentences that were meant for couples to complete and define. I eventually listened to the Lord and got out of bed around three a.m. I began to scribble out the details of the dream. When I finished, I went back to bed.

Several years ago my husband and I, were asked by our church to implement a pre-marriage counseling program. With very little notice, we scrambled to put together a biblically sound program that we felt would lay a great foundation on which to build a marriage. At the time we had been married about twenty-eight years and had walked through each phase of life for the most part. We were given a program the church had just purchased and were asked to review it. Our pastor, Lee Cummings, left it up to us if we wanted to use it. We reviewed the program and felt we could use it if we added supplement materials. We offer this class at our church twice a year now. Any couple who plans on marrying at our church must complete this nine-week course. This course is now called Marital Foundations.

The second time we were teaching this class was when I had the dream I just mentioned. The next morning as I reviewed my scribbles, the Lord began to impress upon me what this was all about. Pre-nuptial agreements are becoming common place, not only for the secular world but also for believers. Couples are using this agreement as their foundation for marriage. The agreement often says, "If this does not work out, this is what we each get." An insurance policy is put in place so each individual walks away feeling they were not ripped off monetarily or materially. How much better would it have been for these couples to make a promise or covenant that they could build their marriage upon. This would be a promise to each other made of foundational stones to enable marriage to be a success and reflect Jesus and His bride. Instead of "our promise to one another," I think a better phrase would be, "our covenant to one another." When I think of the word *promise* today, I realize how our society has misused the word to the point it has no meaning. People break their promises all the time; however, the word *covenant* is not part of our daily language. I believe the word *covenant* will have a bigger impact if it is used. Of course, this is the word the Bible uses. A covenant is a pledge or a promise between two people that is permanent. God made a promise, a covenant with Noah and all future generations by putting a sign in the sky, something to remind us of that covenant. Never again would He destroy the whole earth with a flood.

> "Thus I establish My covenant with you: Never again shall all flesh be cut off by the waters of the flood; never again shall there be a flood to destroy the earth." And God said: "This is the sign of the covenant which I make between Me and you, and every living creature that is with you, for perpetual generations: "I set My rainbow in the cloud, and it shall be for the sign of the covenant between Me and the earth." "It shall be, when I bring a cloud over the earth, that the rainbow shall be seen in the cloud; "and I will remember My covenant which is between Me and you and every living creature of all flesh; the waters shall never again become a flood to destroy all flesh. "The rainbow shall be in the cloud, and I will look on it to remember the everlasting covenant between God and every living creature of all flesh that is on the earth." And God said to Noah, "This is the sign of the covenant which I have established between Me and all flesh that is on the earth."
>
> Genesis 9:11-16 (NKJV)

Our prayer and encouragement would be for all couples to write out "Our Covenant to One Another." It's something tangible to pick up and read, a reminder of foundational stones put in place to protect each other and your marriage. The Lord gave us a covenant sign with the rainbow, our visible sign to remind us of our covenant with the Creator. Wouldn't it be great for us as couples to have a *sign* for one another, which we could look at, read, and remind ourselves of our covenant to each other?

This covenant is best written prior to marriage but can be implemented at anytime. Dan and I counsel with many couples whose marriages are in shambles, and "Our Covenant to One Another" is one of the tools we use to help them get back on track.

The following manual is a tool to help aid couples with writing a covenant to one another for their marriage. There are eighteen stones in this manual, which when defined should set a great foundation in place for every couple to stand upon. When I studied the meaning of the number eighteen, I discovered:

> The number eighteen (*chai*) is considered the completion or fulfillment of the Torah and the commandments (*mitzvot*), to live by or should live by them. This is the will of God, and when a person keeps a commandment it gives God pleasure (*nachat ruach*). The merit of the commandments is long life (*arichut yamim*). This corresponds to eighteen (*chai*).[1]
>
> The number eighteen can also encompass the meaning: to put on, overcome, set boundaries.[2]

**When you study the biblical meanings of numbers, there are positive and negative meanings to numbers. I chose to focus on the positive meaning of eighteen.

A foundation is a solid understructure upon which the rest of the house or building is secured. Foundations are meant to be built or laid once. If the foundation is weak or faulty, the cracks must be repaired, or the entire foundation must be demolished and a new foundation laid or reconstructed.

"To what were its foundations fastened? Or who laid its cornerstone" (Job 38:6, NKJV). In Job 38, the Lord is questioning Job in reference to Himself. The Lord Himself was the foundation upon which all of creation was spoken into being. This massive creation has been held together by the Lord Himself and continues to exist because the foundation is an unshakeable one. Foundations in marriage are weak or unstable when not built on the guidelines of the Word of God. Zechariah gives us some insight as to why foundations are weak, cracked, or crumbling.

> For the idols speak delusion; the diviners envision lies, and tell false dreams; they comfort in vain. Therefore the people wend their way like sheep; *they are in trouble because there is no shepherd.*
>
> Zechariah 10:2 (NKJV)

> Sow for yourselves righteousness; reap in mercy; break up your fallow ground, for it is time to seek the LORD, till He comes and rains righteousness on you. You have plowed wickedness; you have reaped iniquity. *You have eaten the fruit of lies, Because you trusted in your own way, In the multitude of your mighty men.*
>
> Hosea 10:12-13 (NKJV)

Lack of knowledge is another reason for weak foundations.

> My people are destroyed for lack of knowledge. Because you have rejected knowledge, I also will reject you from being priest for Me; because you have forgotten the law of your God, I also will forget your children.
>
> Hosea 4:6 (NKJV)

Our society has bought into the lies that are portrayed when it comes to the role of husband and wife. We have allowed others, Hollywood, media, movies, and TV to shape the identity of husband and wife; we have literally fallen into sin (Isaiah 30:13, NKJV, "Therefore this iniquity shall be to you like a breach ready to fall, a bulge in a high wall, Whose breaking comes suddenly, in an instant"). The good news is we can turn to the Word of God, follow the good examples of godly mentors, and sit under pastors who teach the truth of the Word of God and are truly biblical shepherds. Thank God for His mercy and grace, because regardless if we started with a weak foundation, the Lord always makes a way for those who are truly willing to seek Him.

If you are looking to reestablish a Godly foundation, we encourage you to break up your fallow ground. There is no day like today to begin establishing an unshakeable foundation to build a marriage upon. "For He says: 'In an acceptable time I have heard you, And in the day of salvation I have helped you.' *Behold, now is the accepted time; behold, now is the day of salvation*" (2 Corinthians 6:2, NKJV). Yes, let us build on Jesus Christ, the Chief Cornerstone. "Having been built on the foundation of the apostles and prophets, Jesus Christ Himself being the chief cornerstone, in whom the whole building, being joined together, grows into a holy temple in the Lord" (Ephesians 2:20-21, NKJV).

> Then the LORD replied: *Write down the revelation and make it plain on tablets* so that a herald may run with it. For the revelation awaits an appointed time; it speaks of the end and will not prove false. Though it linger, wait for it; it will certainly come and will not delay.
>
> Habakkuk 2:2-3 (NIV)

We Believe Marriage Is

> Through wisdom a house is built, and by understanding it is established; by knowledge the rooms are filled with all precious and pleasant riches.
>
> Proverbs 24:3-4 (NKJV)

The definition of marriage[3] according to the *Webster's Dictionary* is: "The state of being married; wedlock; the act of marrying or the ceremony entered into by a man and woman so as to live together as husband and wife." To me that sounds more like the definition of a wedding.

When I married my husband, Dan, I didn't even think about what marriage is and how I would describe it. I thought, *I'll work hard to make this last, and if it doesn't, at least I tried*. I thought it was supposed to be forever, but looking around me I realized this was not the case in our society today.

My parents were married for fifty-five years before my dad passed away; however, when I was a senior in high school, my parents dropped the bomb shell that my dad had been married prior to my mother; very shocking, I must say.

The Bible, our manual for life, defines for us what marriage is. Let's take a look at what the Bible has to say about marriage. I believe this will aid you as a couple to be able to come up with your definition of what you believe marriage is. Of course, your definition should line up with the Word of God. We do challenge you to put the definition of marriage into your own words as a couple. Set the first foundational stone. Marriage can be viewed as a spiritual union where both partners are joined together as one through God.

> Therefore a man shall leave his father and mother and be joined to his wife, *and they shall become one flesh.*
>
> Genesis 2:24 (NKJV)

In the King James Version it says: "And shall *cleave* unto his wife" (Genesis 2:24, KJV). The word *cleave*[4] means: "To cling to or adhere to, abide fast, cleave fast together, follow close and hard after, be joined together, keep fast, overtake, pursue hard, stick to, take, catch by pursuit, *cement together*, to stick like glue, *welded together* so that the two cannot be separated without damage to both."

When something is cemented or welded together, it is one. It would take a great deal of major demolition equipment to separate or destroy it.

Cleaving is a wholehearted spiritual commitment that overflows into every area of our being to include the intellectual, emotional, and physical areas. Anything that brings the two of you together and solidifies your relationship more firmly will be cleaving. Whatever puts distance or separation between you mentally, physically, or spiritually must be avoided because it breaks the divine union for marriage God intended.[5]

Becoming one is only possible because of the Creator. Left to ourselves it is an impossible task to ever become one with another person. This is a profound mystery (read Ephesians 5:32). Whenever the Lord established a covenant in the Bible, it was meant to be permanent, lasting, and irrevocable (read Genesis 9:11-17).

God declares two are better than one, and He meant it as one flesh.

> Two are better than one, because they have a good reward for their labor. For if they fall, one will lift up his companion. But woe to him who is alone when he falls, for he has no one to help him up. Again, if two lie down together, they will keep warm; but how can one be warm alone? Though one may be overpowered by another, two can withstand him. *And a threefold cord is not quickly broken.*
>
> Ecclesiastes 4:9-12 (NKJV)

Study the pictures of the ropes. The top rope illustrated is a straight piece of rope. In the second example of rope, the left end of the rope has been unwound to reveal the rope has three parts wound together. Imagine each separate piece of rope representing God, husband, and wife. A threefold cord is not quickly broken. It would be impossible for human hands to tear apart a threefold cord. The three ropes at the bottom of the picture reveals that we can make this rope take on many different shapes; however, it is still the same rope.

One of the more common uses for a rope is to bind things together and give them strength, not allowing what it is holding together to come apart. Another use would be to pull things that are attached to the rope; we are able to do this because the rope can take the weight. Ropes represent strength. Individual marriages may look different from the outside because we all have different temperaments, but the *rope* remains the rope. Throughout marriage, as we grow and mature, the marriage may take on different shapes, but it is the same *rope*. First Corinthians 12:12-31 describes the church as one body with many parts. Marriage is also one body with many parts representing the individuals' uniqueness but remaining as one. The strength of a marriage is a threefold principle, God, husband, and wife. The threefold cord is not quickly broken.

Fill in the blank. The threefold purpose for the marriage union is:

Genesis 1:28; 2:20-24

_____

Genesis 2:24; Hebrews 13:4; 1 Corinthians 7:2-5

_____

Genesis 1:27-28; Psalm 127-128; Proverbs 22:6

_____

In Ephesians 5:21-33 we read that the husband and wife are given a holy charge. The purity of unconditional *agape* love is woven through this scripture with the picture of how Jesus Christ loves His church. Agape love is non-partial in nature; it knows no end, as it exhibits the selfless spiritual character of Christ Jesus. Agape love cannot be destroyed or crushed, it endures forever. These verses declare the profound mystery of husband and wife comparable to Jesus and His bride. *Agape* love for one another will hold a couple together when other loves wax and wane. This love is the same love Jesus loves His church with.

The following are additional scriptures on marriage. These scriptures may be used throughout this manual as an added resource. You will also want to utilize these scriptures as you define what you believe marriage is.

> So God created man in His own image; in the image of God He created him; male and female He created them. Then God blessed them, and God said to them, "Be fruitful and multiply; fill the earth and subdue it; have dominion over the fish of the sea, over the birds of the air, and over every living thing that moves on the earth."
>
> Genesis 1:27-28 (NKJV)

> So Adam gave names to all cattle, to the birds of the air, and to every beast of the field. But for Adam there was not found a helper comparable to him. And the LORD God caused a deep sleep to fall on Adam, and he slept; and He took one of his ribs, and closed up the flesh in its place. Then the rib which the LORD God had taken from man He made into a woman, and He brought her to the man. And Adam said: "This is now bone of my bones and flesh of my flesh; she shall be called Woman, because she was taken out of Man." Therefore a man shall leave his father and mother and be joined to his wife, and they shall become one flesh.
>
> Genesis 2:20-24 (NKJV)

You shall not commit adultery.

Exodus 20:14 (NKJV)

But Ruth said: "Entreat me not to leave you, or to turn back from following after you; for wherever you go, I will go; and wherever you lodge, I will lodge; your people shall be my people, and your God, my God. Where you die, I will die, And there will I be buried. The Lord do so to me, and more also, If anything but death parts you and me."

Ruth 1:16-17 (NKJV)

Houses and riches are an inheritance from fathers, but a prudent wife is from the Lord.

Proverbs 19:14 (NKJV)

Train up a child in the way he should go, and when he is old he will not depart from it.

Proverbs 22:6 (NKJV)

Live joyfully with the wife whom you love all the days of your vain life which He has given you under the sun, all your days of vanity; for that is your portion in life, and in the labor which you perform under the sun.

Ecclesiastes 9:9 (NKJV)

You have heard that it was said to those of old, "You shall not commit adultery." But I say to you that whoever looks at a woman to lust for her has already committed adultery with her in his heart.

Matthew 5:27-28 (NKJV)

The Pharisees also came to Him, testing Him, and saying to Him, "Is it lawful for a man to divorce his wife for just any reason?" And He answered and said to them, "Have you not read that He who made them at the beginning 'made them male and female,' and said, 'For this reason a man shall leave his father and mother and be joined to his wife, and the two shall become one flesh'? So then, they are no longer two but one flesh. Therefore what God has joined together, let not man separate." They said to Him, "Why then did Moses command to give a certificate of divorce, and to put her away?" He said to them, "Moses, because of the hardness of your hearts, permitted you to divorce your wives, but from the beginning it was not so. And I say to you, whoever divorces his wife, except for sexual immorality, and marries another, commits adultery; and whoever marries her who is divorced commits adultery."

Matthew 19:3-9 (NKJV)

Therefore what God has joined together, let not man separate.

Mark 10:9 (NKJV)

Nevertheless, because of sexual immorality, let each man have his own wife, and let each woman have her own husband. Let the husband render to his wife the affection due her, and likewise also the wife to her husband. The wife does not have authority over her own body, but the husband does. And likewise the husband does not have authority over his own body, but the wife does. Do not deprive one another except with consent for a time, that you may give yourselves to fasting and prayer; and come together again so that Satan does not tempt you because of your lack of self-control.

1 Corinthians 7:2-5 (NKJV)

Now to the married I command, yet not I but the Lord: a wife is not to depart from her husband. But even if she does depart, let her remain unmarried or be reconciled to her husband. And a husband is not to divorce his wife. But to the rest I, not the Lord, say: if any brother has a wife who does not believe, and she is willing to live with him, let him not divorce her. And a woman who has a husband who does not believe, if he is willing to live with her, let her not divorce him. For the unbelieving husband is sanctified by the wife, and the unbelieving wife is sanctified by the husband; otherwise your children would be unclean, but now they are holy. But if the unbeliever departs, let him depart; a brother or a sister is not under bondage in such cases. But God has called us to peace.

1 Corinthians 7:10-15 (NKJV)

Submitting to one another in the fear of God. Wives, submit to your own husbands, as to the Lord. For the husband is head of the wife, as also Christ is head of the church; and He is the Savior of the body. Therefore, just as the church is subject to Christ, so let the wives be to their own husbands in everything. Husbands, love your wives, just as Christ also loved the church and gave Himself for her, that He might sanctify and cleanse her with the washing of water by the word, that He might present her to Himself a glorious church, not having spot or wrinkle or any such thing, but that she should be holy and without blemish. So husbands ought to love their own wives as their own bodies; he who loves his wife loves himself. For no one ever hated his own flesh, but nourishes and cherishes it, just as the Lord does the church. For we are members of His body, of His flesh and of His bones "For this reason a man shall leave his father and mother and be joined to his wife, and the two shall become one flesh." This is a great mystery, but I speak concerning Christ and the church. Nevertheless let each one of you in particular so love his own wife as himself, and let the wife see that she respects her husband.

Ephesians 5:21-33 (NKJV)

The older women likewise, that they be reverent in behavior, not slanderers, not given to much wine, teachers of good things; that they admonish the young women to love their husbands, to love their children, to be discreet, chaste, homemakers, good, obedient to their own husbands, that the word of God may not be blasphemed.

Titus 2:3-5 (NKJV)

Marriage is honorable among all, and the bed undefiled; but fornicators and adulterers God will judge.

Hebrews 13:4 (NKJV)

Also look up 1 Peter 3:1-17, Psalm 127-128 and Proverbs 31, as you read these passages, reflect upon how they can be applied to married life.

Foundational Stone One

As a couple, write out in your own words: *We believe marriage is:*

_____

_____

_____

_____

_____

_____

_____

_____

_____

_____

_____

Our Doctrinal Statement of Faith

> All Scripture is given by inspiration of God, and is profitable for doctrine, for reproof, for correction, for instruction in righteousness.
>
> 2 Timothy 3:16 (NKJV)

Knowing what we believe and why we believe the way we do is an essential foundational stone. For marriages to be strong and at peace, differences in doctrine must not keep us at arm's length. Conversations that are meant to bring us closer should not drive a wedge between us spiritually. We have counseled with many couples who are not in agreement when it comes to their spiritual walk with the Lord. These couples marry with the idea that the spiritual aspect of marriage will work itself out. Once these couples have been married a few years, they find themselves longing to return to the traditions, beliefs, and church environment they grew up in. We have counseled with couples who did not know what church they were going to attend once they married (they each attended their own church). Nor did they know how they were going to raise their children in the future in regard to belief. We encourage couples in this situation to work this issue out before they marry and come to terms with their beliefs. We encourage them to write out their own doctrinal statement of faith.

The Bible gives us some absolutes in regard to marriage. If you are single and considering marriage, the Bible is clear when it says, "Do not be unequally yoked together with unbelievers. For what fellowship has righteousness with lawlessness? And what communion has light with darkness?" (2 Corinthians 6:14, NKJV). The Bible also gives directions to believers who are married to unbelievers.

> But to the rest I, not the Lord, say: If any brother has a wife who does not believe, and she is willing to live with him, let him not divorce her. And a woman who has a husband who does not believe, if he is willing to live with her, let her not divorce him. For the unbelieving husband is sanctified by the wife, and the unbelieving wife is sanctified by the husband; otherwise your children would be unclean, but now they are holy. But if the unbeliever departs, let him depart; a brother or a sister is not under bondage in such cases. But God has called us to peace. For how do you know, O wife, whether you will save your husband? Or how do you know, O husband, whether you will save your wife? But as God has distributed to each one, as the Lord has called each one, so let him walk. And so I ordain in all the churches.
>
> 1 Corinthians 7:12-17 (NKJV)

When you individually examine your own beliefs, writing out your own personal testimony may give you insight into why you believe what you believe. After you have given much thought to your beliefs as an individual, come together as a couple and take a look at your agreements as well as differences. For couples who grew up in the same church or with similar backgrounds, this may be an easy task. But for the couples whose backgrounds were spiritually different, this may pose a challenge. In either case, this is well worth the effort when considering you are spending a lifetime together. For couples who are already married, writing out your doctrinal statement of faith will strengthen you, bring you closer together, and give you a great foundation as you raise your children and encourage their faith.

I accepted Jesus Christ as my Savior as a young girl. My family did not attend church; however, I would walk down to the local Baptist church each Sunday for church service and Monday after school for Pioneer Girls, which is a faith-based Bible club for young girls in elementary school. I also attended vacation Bible school at Pleasant Hill Bible Church each summer. I am eternally grateful for the pastors of these churches as well as other adults who invested in my life as a young girl. Because of their faithfulness to the Lord, my name is written in the Lamb's Book of Life. You can never underestimate the value of children's programs at local churches; I am an eternal result of such programs.

Much of my foundational beliefs came from these churches I attended as a young girl. I grew and matured in the Lord through various means or avenues of the Lord and His leading. The Holy Spirit always leads us to a deeper, more insightful relationship with Him if we respond to His promptings. The above was a brief introduction of my salvation experience. Writing a detailed testimony will enhance a revelation on why you believe what you believe. Why do you believe what you believe? The questions below should be very helpful as you ponder your story and make it part of your story together as a couple.

We Promise

Another suggestion for a good place to start when endeavoring to write a doctrinal statement of faith could be reviewing your church's statement of faith. The church you attend will have a doctrinal statement of faith. Normally when you become a member at a church, this statement of faith is given to you. Many churches have membership classes you must attend prior to becoming a member, and the statement of faith is covered during this class. Another great place for finding statements of faith is on church websites.

Answering the following questions and reading the scriptures provided should help you as you write a statement of faith together as a couple. The listed scriptures below are not all-inclusive, but for your resource. These scriptures are reflective of my beliefs.

Individual:

- I accepted Jesus Christ as my Lord Savior and King:

    _____

    _____

    _____

- My faith has grown in the following ways:

    _____

    _____

    _____

- I seek the Lord in the following ways:

    _____

    _____

    _____

- When I am faced with a crisis, I seek the Lord in the following ways:

  _____

  _____

  _____

- The biggest change in my life since accepting Jesus Christ as my Savior has been:

  _____

  _____

  _____

- The biggest challenge in my life since accepting Jesus Christ as my Savior has been:

  _____

  _____

  _____

Couple:[6]

- We believe the Bible is (2 Timothy 3:15-16, 1 Thessalonians 2:13, 2 Peter 1:21):

  _____

  _____

We Promise

- We believe the Godhead is (Deuteronomy 6:4, Matthew 28:19, Mark 12:29, John 1:1, John 1:14, 18, John 14:28, 15:26, 16:28, 2 Corinthians 13:14, Philippians 2:6):

_____

_____

_____

- We believe the following about the deity (Isaiah 7:14, Matthew 1:23, Luke 24:39, Acts 1:9, Acts 2:22, 10:38, Romans 8:34, Ephesians 4:8-10, 1 Corinthians 15:22-24, 51-57, 2 Corinthians 5:21, 1 Thessalonians 4:13-18, Hebrews 7:25-26, 1 Peter 2:22, Revelation 20:1-6):

_____

_____

_____

- We believe man's fall, redemption, and salvation is (Genesis 1:26-31, 3:1-7, John 3:3-6, Romans 3:10, 3:23, 5:12-21, Romans 10:8-15, 1 Corinthians 15:3-4, 2 Corinthians 7:10, Ephesians 2:8, James 1:18, 1 Peter 1:23, 1 John 5:1,12):

_____

_____

_____

- We believe water baptism is (Matthew 28:19, Acts 2:38-39, 8:36-39, 10:47-48, Romans 6:4, Colossians 2:12):

  _____

  _____

  _____

- We believe in the baptism of the Holy Spirit (Matthew 3:11, John 14:16-17, Acts 1:4-8, 2:4-38, 10:44-46, 11:14-16, 19:1-7):

  _____

  _____

  _____

- We believe in the gifts of the Holy Spirit (1 Corinthians 12:4-11, 28; Ephesians 4:7-16):

  _____

  _____

  _____

- We believe in holiness (1 Peter 1:14-16, Hebrews 12:14, 1 Thessalonians 5:23, 1 John 2:6):

  _____

  _____

  _____

We Promise

- We believe in divine healing (Isaiah. 53:4-5, Matthew 8:16-17, Mark 16:18, James 5:13-25, 1 Peter 2:24):

  _____

  _____

  _____

- We believe in the Lord's Supper (Luke 22:14-20, 1 Corinthians 11:20-34):

  _____

  _____

  _____

- We believe in the resurrection of man (Daniel 12:2-3, Matthew 25:46, John 5:28-29, Acts 1:11, 1 Corinthians 15:22-24, 1 Thessalonians 4:16-17, 2 Thessalonians 1:9, Rev. 20:10-15):

  _____

  _____

  _____

- We believe in hell and eternity (Hebrews 9:27, Revelation 19:20):

  _____

  _____

  _____

Additional questions for you to ponder and work on as a couple:

- Are we at the same spiritual level? If not, are we willing to reach and fulfill our potential in Christ Jesus?

  _____

- Do we have the same doctrinal background? And if not, how will these doctrinal differences impact our relationship and family?

  _____

  _____

  _____

- Do we both believe in the born-again experience?

  _____

- How do we view the spiritual gifts and their influence for today?

  _____

- Do we both believe in speaking in tongues? Is this for today, and will it enhance our walk with the Lord?

  _____

- Are we both willing to obey God no matter what?

  _____

- Do we both believe God's way is the best way?

  _____

We Promise

- Is prayer a vital part of both of our lives?

  _____

- Do we both confess our sins on a regular basis?

  _____

- How do we each feel in regard to drinking alcohol?

  _____

- How do we both feel in regard to smoking?

  _____

Additional scriptures for you to ponder on being equally yoked:

> And what accord has Christ with Belial? Or what part has a believer with an unbeliever? And what agreement has the temple of God with idols? For you are the temple of the living God. As God has said: "I will dwell in them and walk among them. I will be their God, and they shall be My people. Therefore come out from among them and be separate, says the Lord. Do not touch what is unclean, And I will receive you. I will be a Father to you, And you shall be My sons and daughters, says the Lord Almighty.
> 2 Corinthians 6:15-18 (NKJV)

> Therefore, having these promises, beloved, let us cleanse ourselves from all filthiness of the flesh and spirit, perfecting holiness in the fear of God.
> 2 Corinthians 7:1 (NKJV)

> And I will make you swear by the Lord, the God of heaven and the God of the earth, that you will not take a wife for my son from the daughters of the Canaanites, among whom I dwell; but you shall go to my country and to my family, and take a wife for my son Isaac.
> Genesis 24:3-4 (NKJV)

Penny and Rev. Dr. Daniel Loosenort

I wrote to you in my epistle not to keep company with sexually immoral people.

1 Corinthians 5:9 (NKJV)

Therefore do not be partakers with them. For you were once darkness, but now you are light in the Lord. Walk as children of light (for the fruit of the Spirit is in all goodness, righteousness, and truth), finding out what is acceptable to the Lord.

Ephesians 5:7-10 (NKJV)

Foundational Stone Two

As a couple write out in your own words: *Our doctrinal statement of faith is:*

_____

_____

_____

_____

_____

_____

_____

_____

_____

_____

I Now Pronounce You Husband and Wife

> I, therefore, the prisoner of the Lord, beseech you to walk worthy of the calling with which you were called.
>
> Ephesians 4:1 (NKJV)

The pronouncement of husband and wife will thrust us into an adventure whether we are ready or not for the lifetime commitment of the endless relationship. When we were children we played the game of hide and seek. We counted to ten and yelled, "Ready or not, here I come." Many couples embark on marriage the same way, playing a game of hide and seek encounters. They charge in, hoping to find a lasting relationship, even if both individuals have not made proper preparation. Standing at the altar of matrimony, they wonder what they will find instead of knowing what they have found.

A mandate is given to us as we live out our lives in whatever circumstances we are in ("Let each one remain in the same calling in which he was called." 1 Corinthians 7:20, NKJV); married or single, we are to obey and follow the example of the Word of God and Christ Jesus.

> Now what I am commanding you today *is not too difficult for you or beyond your reach*. It is not up in heaven, so that you have to ask, "Who will ascend into heaven to get it and proclaim it to us so we may obey it?" Nor is it beyond the sea, so that you have to ask, "Who will cross the sea to get it and proclaim it to us so we may obey it?" No, *the word is very near you; it is in your mouth and*

in your heart so you may obey it. See, I set before you today life and prosperity, death and destruction. For I command you today to love the Lord your God, *to walk in his ways*, and to keep his commands, decrees and laws; then you will live and increase, and the Lord your God will bless you in the land you are entering to possess.

Deuteronomy 30:11-15 (NIV)

How could it be humanly possible for man or woman to live up to such a mandate fulfilling the roles the Lord has called them to as husband and wife? God will never call us to do anything without giving us the means to fully equip ourselves, to fulfill the mandate He has called us to achieve. Ephesians chapter two is a great reminder of what the Lord will enable us to do.

> For we are His workmanship, created in Christ Jesus for good works, which God prepared beforehand that we should walk in them.
>
> Ephesians 2:10 (NKJV)

In Corinthians it says:

> Or do you not know that your body is the temple of the Holy Spirit who is in you, whom you have from God, and *you are not your own*? For you were bought at a price; therefore glorify God in your body and in your spirit, which are God's.
>
> 1 Corinthians 6:19-20 (NKJV)

These verses are followed in chapter seven by charges given to the husband and wife:

- Man should not touch a woman (implying unless it is his wife).
- Husband to give wife affection (kindness, goodwill).
- Wife also to give husband affection.
- Wife and husband do not have authority over their own bodies (they are one).
- Husband and wife are not to deprive one another sexual pleasure except for a time of fasting and prayer, so that they do not fall into temptation.

Mutual submission is the biblical emphasis as stated in 1 Corinthians 7 (see above bullets) and in Ephesians 5. "Submitting to one another in the fear of God" (Ephesians 5:21, NKJV).

We Promise

When we became a child of the King, we received an inheritance that would enable us to fulfill the mandate the Lord has called us to. The following verses should further stress this point.

> In Him also we have obtained an inheritance, being predestined according to the purpose of Him who works all things according to the counsel of His will.
>
> Ephesians 1:11 (NKJV)

> The eyes of your understanding being enlightened; that you may know what is the hope of His calling, what are the riches of the glory of His inheritance in the saints.
>
> Ephesians 1:18 (NKJV)

> Giving thanks to the Father who has qualified us to be partakers of the inheritance of the saints in the light.
>
> Colossians 1:12 (NKJV)

> To an inheritance incorruptible and undefiled and that does not fade away, reserved in heaven for you.
>
> 1 Peter 1:4 (NKJV)

Our God has declared, "All things are possible!"
Read the following verses and fill in the blanks.

Matthew 19:26, *With men this is:*

_____

Mark 9:23, *If you can believe*:

_____

Mark 10:27, *With men it is impossible:*

_____

Luke 18:27, *Are impossible with men:*

_____

I believe those verses were not just reserved for miracles, signs, and wonders but also for how we conduct our lives on a daily basis. John 15 shows us we can ask of the Father anything, and it is followed up by "that you love one another."

> You did not choose Me, but I chose you and appointed you that you should *go and bear fruit*, and *that your fruit should remain*, that *whatever you ask* the Father in My name *He may give you*. These things I command you, *that you love one another*.
>
> John 15:16-17 (NKJV)

Fill in the following blanks:

- …go and

___

- …that your

___

- …that whatever you ask

___

- …that you

___

What better place could we bear fruit than with our spouse and immediate family members? If we ask of the Father to enable and teach us to be a godly husband or wife, fulfilling the roles He has called us to, we know that is according to His will.

> Now this is the confidence that we have in Him, *that if we ask anything according to His will*, He hears us and if we know that He hears us, *whatever we ask, we know that we have the petitions that we have asked of Him*.
>
> 1 John 5:14-15 (NKJV)

Even when we are tempted to be selfish and desire our own way, God has made a way for us. "No temptation has overtaken you except such as is common to man; but God is faithful, who will not allow you to be tempted beyond what you are able, but with the temptation will also make the way of escape, that you may be able to bear it" (1 Corinthians 10:13, NKJV).

Husbands and wives, even if you feel you have messed it up, God in His grace and mercy always gives us the opportunity to make amends through repentance. We will discuss the true meaning of repentance later in this manual. I encourage you whether you are engaged or already married to throw off anything that will keep you from fulfilling your role as the husband or wife God has called you to be.

> Therefore, since we are surrounded by such a great cloud of witnesses, *let us throw off everything that hinders and the sin that so easily entangles*, and let us run with perseverance the race marked out for us. Let us fix our eyes on Jesus, the author and perfecter of our faith, who for the joy set before him endured the cross, scorning its shame, and sat down at the right hand of the throne of God. Consider him who endured such opposition from sinful men, so that you will not grow weary and lose heart.
>
> Hebrews 12:1-3 (NIV)

Do you believe God will fully equip you to fulfill your role as husband or wife? Then let's press forward, putting foundational stones in place.

> Do all things without complaining and disputing, that you may become blameless and harmless, children of God without fault in the midst of a crooked and perverse generation, among whom you shine as lights in the world, holding fast the word of life, so that I may rejoice in the day of Christ that I have not run in vain or labored in vain.
>
> Philippians 2:14-16 (NKJV)

The Role of the Husband

> Husbands, love your wives, just as Christ also loved the church and gave Himself for her.
>
> Ephesians 5:25 (NKJV)

For the sake of clarity, I would like to make a differentiation between roles and responsibilities (in regard to this manual). A role is a position one takes (this will be unchangeable), whereas responsibility is being in charge of (completing the task at hand) certain aspects or household duties when it comes to marriage (this may change throughout a marriage). I have found we like to interchange these two words when it comes to defining the role of the husband or wife. I will be touching base on responsibilities in marriage later in this manual. I have endeavored to stick with the role of the husband in this section; however, to bring better clarification in regard to the role of the husband, I found it necessary to cover some aspects of the wife's role also. Therefore, women will also need to study this section, and men will also need to study the section on the role of a wife in marriage. The Bible has clearly stated the two shall become one, so when revealing information in regard to the roles, it is difficult to separate some aspects.

Now that we have laid some ground work that reassures us, God will enable us to fulfill our roles as husband and wife, let's look at what God has mandated the husband to fulfill; the third foundational stone or principle.

Men, the Lord commanded you to love your wife just as Jesus loves the church. Wow, what a mandate; this charge God has given to the husband. I don't know a woman alive who wouldn't do flips for a man who would love her as Christ loves His church! Plus, He gave himself for her!

In Genesis, when God created the earth, after each creation He declared it good. However, in Genesis 2:18, God said man should have a companion and not be alone. The foundation for different roles started as a permanent fact of creation, not based on culture, before sin came in and warped our concepts of husband and wife. The roles of man and wife were corrupted by the fall, not created by God. Jesus restored "all" through His death and resurrection, making a way for us to fulfill our God-given roles. Common knowledge for years now has revealed that Christian marriage has the same divorce rate as the secular world. How can this be, if we as believers have been qualified to do His will?[7]

Read the following scriptures so as to lay more ground work to unpack the role of the husband.

> Then God blessed *them*, and God said to *them*, *"Be fruitful and multiply; fill the earth and subdue it; have dominion over the* fish of the sea, over the birds of the air, and over every living thing that moves on the earth." And God said, "See, I have given you every herb that yields seed which is on the face of all the earth, and every tree whose fruit yields seed; to you it shall be for food.

"Also, to every beast of the earth, to every bird of the air, and to everything that creeps on the earth, in which there is life, I have given every green herb for food"; and it was so.

Genesis 1:28-30 (NKJV)

To the woman He said: "I will greatly multiply your sorrow and your conception; in pain you shall bring forth children; your desire shall be for your husband, *and he shall rule over you.*" Then to Adam He said, "Because you have heeded the voice of your wife, and have eaten from the tree of which I commanded you, saying, 'You shall not eat of it': Cursed is the ground for your sake; in toil you shall eat of it all the days of your life. Both thorns and thistles it shall bring forth for you, and you shall eat the herb of the field. In the sweat of your face you shall eat bread till you return to the ground, for out of it you were taken; for dust you are, and to dust you shall return."

Genesis 3:16-19 (NKJV)

You have heard that it was said to those of old, "You shall not commit adultery." But I say to you that *whoever looks at a woman to lust for her has already committed adultery with her in his heart.*

Matthew 5:27-28 (NKJV)

But I want you to know that the *head of every man is Christ, the head of woman is man,* and the head of Christ is God.

1 Corinthians 11:3 (NKJV)

Submitting to one another in the fear of God. Wives, submit to your own husbands, as to the Lord. For *the husband is head of the wife*, as also Christ is head of the church; and He is the Savior of the body. Therefore, just as the church is subject to Christ, so let the wives be to their own husbands in everything. *Husbands, love your wives, just as Christ also loved the church and gave Himself for her, that He might sanctify and cleanse her with the washing of water by the word, that He might present her to Himself a glorious church, not having spot or wrinkle or any such thing, but that she should be holy and without blemish. So husbands ought to love their own wives as their own bodies; he who loves his wife loves himself. For no one ever hated his own flesh, but nourishes and cherishes it, just as the Lord does the church.* For we are members of His body, of His flesh and of His bones. "For this reason a *man shall leave his father and mother* and be *joined to his wife, and the two shall become one flesh.*" This is a great mystery, but I speak concerning Christ and the church. Nevertheless *let each one of you in particular so love his own wife as himself,* and let the wife see that she respects her husband.

Ephesians 5:21-33 (NKJV)

And you, *fathers, do not provoke your children to wrath, but bring them up in the training and admonition of the Lord.*

Ephesians 6:4 (NKJV)

Husbands, love your wives and do not be bitter toward them.

Colossians 3:19 (NKJV)

But if anyone does not provide for his own, and especially for those of his household, he has denied the faith and is worse than an unbeliever.

1 Timothy 5:8 (NKJV)

For even when we were with you, we commanded you this: *If anyone will not work, neither shall he eat.*

2 Thessalonians 3:10 (NKJV)

Husbands, likewise, dwell with them with understanding, giving honor to the wife, as to the weaker vessel, and as being heirs together of the grace of life, that your prayers may not be hindered.

1 Peter 3:7 (NKJV)

Christ's love for the church is unconditional. His love remains constant regardless of what His bride does or does not do. "Jesus Christ is the same yesterday, today, and forever" (Hebrews 13:8, NKJV).

God has called the man to be the (1 Corinthians 11:3):

_____

How do you view headship? In Galatians 3:28, we are considered all the same in Christ Jesus, we are equal. Using Christ as our example, does He treat us all with value and regard? As the head of your home, how can you apply this as you lead?

_____

_____

_____

Fill in the following blanks:

Read Ephesians 5:21-33 (NIV). In the fear of God we are to: _____. The husband is the_____.

Husbands, love your _____ as Christ loves the _____ and He gave _____.

_____ your wife as _____. No one ever hated his own flesh.

But _____ and _____ it.

Ephesians 5:27(NIV) says, "To present her to himself as a _____ church."

When was the last time you saw a woman who was verbally or physically abused as radiant, splendid, or glorious? When you look at a woman and you see her glowing or radiant, it is usually because her husband cherishes, nurtures, and holds her in high esteem. She is radiant because she is treated royally. We have all seen women who look as though they have been dragged through the mud, and it's because they have been.

Read Colossians 3:19 (NIV), filling in the blanks: Husbands, _____ your _____ and do not be _____ toward them.

Read 1 Timothy 5:8 (NIV), filling in the blank: who are we supposed to provide for: _____.

In 1 Peter 3:7 (NIV), husbands are to treat (dwell with) their wives in the following ways so their _____ are not hindered. List the ways you are to treat your wife.

- What does it mean to understand your wife?

_____

_____

_____

- What does it mean to honor your wife?

_____

_____

_____

- What does "your wife is the weaker vessel" mean?

_____

_____

_____

_____

We Promise

- Define in your own words "heir together":

_____

_____

_____

Further study is needed to really appreciate and discover how Christ loves His church, the bride.

Throughout Scripture Jesus Christ is called the King, the King of kings. Let's take a look at these scriptures:

> Which He will manifest in His own time, He who is the blessed and only Potentate, the King of kings and Lord of lords.
>
> 1 Timothy 6:15 (NKJV)

> These will make war with the Lamb, and the Lamb will overcome them, for He is Lord of lords and King of kings; and those who are with Him are called, chosen, and faithful.
>
> Revelation 17:14 (NKJV)

> And He has on His robe and on His thigh a name written: KING OF KINGS AND LORD OF LORDS.
>
> Revelation 19:16 (NKJV)

A king always leads, and Christ Jesus the king leads His church, the bride. He leads by authority, by serving, and is a king who is always welcoming or beckoning His people to come in, loving them unconditionally ("The LORD has appeared of old to me, saying: 'Yes, I have loved you with an everlasting love; Therefore with lovingkindness I have drawn you.'" Jeremiah 31:3, NKJV). This type of love is also identified in 1 John. "My little children, let us not love in word or in tongue, but in deed and in truth" (1 John 3:18, NKJV). A husband is called to lead his bride just as Jesus leads His bride the church; this is done with confidence and the authority Christ has given.

Another facet of this leading is serving. To serve as Christ did, we can look at Scripture for the true revelation of what serving is. In John 13 Christ washed the disciples' feet. In

Philippians, the Bible says Christ took on the very nature of a servant. Leading must always encompass serving and loving. Another part of serving is providing for your wife. "But if anyone does not provide for his own, and especially for those of his household, he has denied the faith and is worse than an unbeliever" (1 Timothy 5:8, NKJV). We are also reminded in 2 Thessalonians, if we are unwilling to work, we will not eat. The Lord expects us to work.

> Then to Adam He said, "Because you have heeded the voice of your wife, and have eaten from the tree of which I commanded you, saying, 'You shall not eat of it.' Cursed is the ground for your sake; *In toil you shall eat of it* all the days of your life."
>
> Genesis 3:17 (NKJV)

One of the extreme needs of a woman is to feel secure. Much of this security comes to her by knowing and experiencing that she will be taken care of, not fearing financial failure. We have counseled many married women who are overburdened with the task of providing for the family. They have played party to enabling their husbands into complacency and role reversal. These types of husbands have not stepped up to the plate and made a serious effort to fulfill their role in regard to provision. Their focus has been self-centered on unfulfilled boyhood dreams of sports, hunting, or dreams of a business venture that has not proven to provide for the family. Please do not misunderstand and think we are classifying all men into this trend. One might contribute some of this dilemma to single-parent homes where the male has not had a male mentor in the provider role.

To further compound this issue, women have fallen into compromise when seeking prospective husbands, or they themselves also may never have experienced a male mentor in the provisional role. We have counseled with women who even prior to marriage have taken on the debt of their fiancé. Some of the common examples would be: buying their own engagement ring, taking over enormous credit card debt of the male, purchasing a home in their name only because the male's credit score is so low, taking over car payments or even paying child support for the male from a previous marriage, and the list could go on (ladies, if you are currently in an engagement with a male such as this, consider it a *red flag* warning, and resolve these issues prior to marriage). The woman was not intended to be the sole provider for the home; she is to be the helpmate. She was not created to hold up under the enormous pressures and responsibilities of the provisional. Left unchecked, these women will burn out or eventually divorce, only to repeat the pattern again because the issues of proper marital roles have not been dealt with. Men, if your financial house is not in order, we encourage you to rectify the financial situation prior to marriage; this will prove your integrity and willingness to be the provider to your fiancée.

Husbands should also be willing to intercede (pray) for their wives just as Jesus intercedes on our behalf. Hebrews 2-13 (look up and read) elaborate on Jesus the High Priest and His intercessions. We will address prayer in more detail later in this manual.

Jesus gave the ultimate for His church; He gave His life, and He sacrificed. One last time, let's visit the following verse. "Husbands, love your wives, just as Christ also loved the church and gave Himself for her" (Ephesians 5:25, NKJV). The willingness to sacrifice for your wife should be paramount; setting aside what you may desire for the welfare and benefit of your wife will be a radiant example of love as Jesus loves.[8]

All the material presented in this chapter should give you a great start in being able to write your promise to your wife, "My role as a husband is…" This is not all-inclusive; there are tremendous resources available to us through other books and the Internet. Some of these resources will be listed under notes at the end of this manual.

Foundational Stone Three

> His love was not cautious but extravagant. He didn't love in order to get something from us but to give everything of himself to us. Love like that"
> Ephesians 5:2 (MSG)

In your own words write, *My role as a husband is:*

_____

_____

_____

_____

_____

_____

_____

_____

> He who finds a wife finds a good thing, and obtains favor from the Lord.
> Proverbs 18:22 (NKJV)

Role of the Wife

> The wise woman builds her house, But the foolish pulls it down with her hands.
> Proverbs 14:1 (NKJV)

The saying goes, "Behind every great man is an even greater woman." I think Louis D. Brandies was tagged for this quote, but I am not certain. As I was searching trying to find out who the author was quoting this, I ran across another quote that my husband favored. "Behind every successful man you'll find a woman who has nothing to wear" (Harold Coffin). Now we will elaborate on this later, but there is a certain amount of truth to that quote, and I am sure the man quoting this was very serious behind his humor. His wife must have grabbed hold of a truth and ran with it full steam ahead.

In our life circumstances as a couple, whenever something is going wrong or is amiss, my husband turns to me and says, "Must be we aren't having enough sex." Now you must understand, these circumstances may have absolutely nothing to do with me. Just as security and provision is a huge issue or need for women, men also have a huge need, and it is for sexual fulfillment. I think if we were to take balancing scales and on one side have man's heaviest (greatest) marital need and woman's heaviest (greatest) marital need, it would certainly be security and provision for her, honor and sexual fulfillment for him. This scale then would be equally balanced.

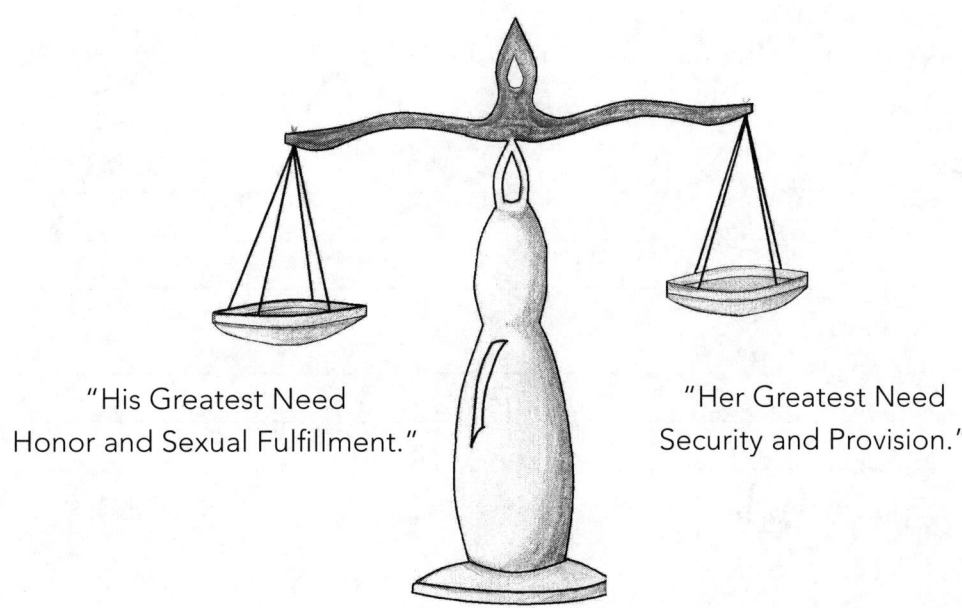

"His Greatest Need Honor and Sexual Fulfillment."

"Her Greatest Need Security and Provision."

Examining the Scriptures will reveal what God has called the woman to fulfill in regard to her role in marriage.

Read the following scriptures and fill in the blanks:

Genesis 2:18 (NKJV), To be a _____ comparable to him (the husband).

The word *helper* in the Hebrew (*ezer, azar*) means: "to surround, protect, aid, succour (to assist in times of great difficulty)," compare to; how the Holy Spirit helps us in times of need.[9]

Ephesians 5:22-24, 1 Peter 3:1-5, Wives are to _____ as unto the Lord.

Your adornment should be: _____

You should possess: _____

Titus 2:4 (NKJV), To _____ your husband.

Titus 2:5 (NKJV), To be _____, _____, _____, _____, _____, that the Word of God may not be blasphemed.

Ephesians 5:33 (NKJV), Let the wife see that she _____ her husband.

1 Timothy 2:15, 5:14 (NKJV), Bear _____, continue in _____, _____, _____, _____.

Genesis 1:28 (NKJV); Be _____, and _____, and _____, and _____, and have _____ (to have dominion means: prevail against, reign, bear, make to rule, overtake).[10]

We Promise

Look up Proverbs 31:10-31 and list at least twenty attributes of a virtuous woman. It may be helpful to read this passage out of The Message Bible.

_____

_____

_____

_____

_____

_____

_____

_____

_____

_____

From the scriptures we have just studied, we can summarize a few roles of the wife. She is to:

- Help
- Submit
- Respect
- Be pure
- Possess a gentle, quiet spirit
- Good mother
- Good homemaker
- Attributes from Proverbs 31

In addition, we find her body is not her own, just as the husband's body is not his own.

Read Genesis 2:25 (NKJV) and fill in the blanks: And they were both _____, the man and his wife, and were not, _____.

> Nevertheless, because of sexual immorality, let each man have his own wife, and let each woman have her own husband. Let the husband render to his wife the affection due her, and likewise also the wife to her husband. The wife does not have authority over her own body, but the husband does. And likewise the husband does not have authority over his own body, but the wife does. *Do not deprive one another except with consent for a time, that you may give yourselves to fasting and prayer; and come together again so that Satan does not tempt you because of your lack of self-control.*
>
> 1 Corinthians 7:2-5 (NKJV)

There are many opinions out there on what a healthy sex life is. We believe according to Scripture we are only to abstain from sex for a time of fasting and prayer. Most people do not fast longer than three days. We are told to come together again so that Satan does not tempt us. Many people assume that it is the woman who does not hold up her end of the deal when it comes to the sexual aspect of marriage. Yes, we counsel many women who purely do not care to have sex; however, we see many women who are sexually frustrated because of their husband's lack of sexual interest. We will discuss sexual issues further in the chapter titled "Ours for the Keeping: Sex and Intimacy."

One of the biggest questions of our day is: should the wife work outside of the home? If she does work outside of the home, how does that affect her responsibilities and role as a wife, and one day, a mother?

I have given much prayer, thought, and study to these questions. I searched many articles already written for the answer to these questions and did not find what would bring agreement to my spirit. So I had to depend upon the Lord to reveal to me what He would have me share with you. I did not find the one answer but did discover what the Lord would reveal to me was the seasons of life.

First off, your role as a wife and mother does not change biblically whether you work or not. However, your responsibilities as a wife and mother do change and will take on a different flavor than if you were in the home full time. The responsibilities of the husband change also when the wife works outside the home, and as the head of the wife, he must be willing to take on more responsibilities and fill in the gaps. He must lighten her load because she is the weaker vessel. He must be the servant, leader, protector, affirmer, cherisher, and supporter God intends him to be, regardless of their circumstances or work statuses. Men, the heavy load is placed on you; she is your helpmate.

Each woman, wife, and mother will go through different seasons of life. With each season will come unique responsibilities of that season. This does not mean it will last a lifetime or a year or six years. Only the Lord and you as a couple will be able to define that season. The world cannot define the Lord's plans and purposes for you and neither can a religious doctrine set up by man; however, all our decisions must be made by the Word of God and not against it.

Ecclesiastes 3:1-8 (NKJV) says,

> To everything there is a season, a time for every purpose under heaven: a time to be born, and a time to die; a time to plant, and a time to pluck what is planted; a time to kill, and a time to heal; a time to break down, and a time to build up; a time to weep, and a time to laugh; a time to mourn, and a time to dance; a time to cast away stones, and a time to gather stones; a time to embrace, and a time to refrain from embracing; a time to gain, and a time to lose; a time to keep, and a time to throw away; a time to tear, and a time to sew; a time to keep silence, and a time to speak; a time to love, and a time to hate; a time of war, and a time of peace.

God has an eternal plan that includes the purposes and activities of every person on this earth. It is vitally important that we give ourselves to God as a holy and living sacrifice, allowing the Holy Spirit to direct and fulfill through us God's perfect will and not miss His timing and purpose for each of us. Studying the following scriptures should reinforce just how much God cares about our future.

> Commit to the Lord whatever you do, and your plans will succeed.
>
> Proverbs 16:3 (NIV)

> When a man's ways please the Lord, He makes even his enemies to be at peace with him.
>
> Proverbs 16:7 (NKJV)

> A man's heart plans his way, but the Lord directs his steps.
>
> Proverbs 16:9 (NKJV)

> Your word is a lamp to my feet And a light to my path.
>
> Psalm 119:105 (NKJV)

> For I know the thoughts that I think toward you, says the Lord, thoughts of peace and not of evil, to give you a future and a hope. Then you will call upon Me and go and pray to Me, and I will listen to you. And you will seek Me and find Me, when you search for Me with all your heart. I will be found by you, says the Lord, and I will bring you back from your captivity; I will gather you from all the nations and from all the places where I have driven you, says the Lord, and I will bring you to the place from which I cause you to be carried away captive.
>
> Jeremiah 29:11-14 (NKJV)

> But seek first the kingdom of God and His righteousness, and all these things shall be added to you.
>
> Matthew 6:33 (NKJV)

> If any of you lacks wisdom, let him ask of God, who gives to all liberally and without reproach, and it will be given to him.
>
> James 1:5 (NKJV)

> For the revelation awaits an appointed time; it speaks of the end and will not prove false. Though it linger, wait for it; it will certainly come and will not delay.
>
> Habakkuk 2:3 (NIV)

Look up and read: Proverbs 3:1-23

How can the verses you just read give you, as a couple, wisdom, and how can they be applied to your future life or current circumstances?

_____

_____

_____

_____

It is the Lord's will that you know His will for your life and your season! Picture in your mind a treadmill. The treadmill represents the world system or a religious doctrinal system, which is adopted by you without your seeking out the truth of the Word of God (when you accept or take on what you have been told by parents, church, or any other organization regardless of whether or not it is truly biblical). When you walk on a treadmill, you are working hard, walking fast, but going nowhere. If you walk on this treadmill long enough, eventually the tread wears off, you slip, fall, and injure yourself. This is not God's plan for you. Do not buy into the world's system or any other system and adopt it as yours! Do not be a man pleaser; be a God pleaser. Do not fear man or man's opinion; fear and revere God. God has a plan and a destination for all seasons of your life. When you seek God for your destinations, you will be going somewhere and fulfilling a purpose, not just walking on a treadmill.

My heart is this: if it is possible for the wife to be home, I believe that is the best place for her, especially when she is raising children, regardless of their ages. I have done this every way in regard to raising children. I have worked full time, part time, worked out of the home, and stayed at home, not producing any type of income. I have obeyed God and disobeyed God when it comes to the work situation. I realize there are fewer and fewer women at home and more and more in the work force for all kinds of reasons. Be sure the reason you are working and where you are working is God's plan for you and for the season you are in. Do not fall into the treadmill trap! Fear God, not man.

I read a book years ago titled *All the Women of the Bible*. I decided to dig it out and review it again. I knew there were women in the Bible who worked. What I was trying to discover was what season of life were they in. What was God's purpose for them in the workplace, and what effect did it have on those around them? This proved to be a great challenge. As far as I could understand, they were married or widowed; some of their children were mentioned, others not. There was no real form of birth control then, so you may assume most likely they had children. As I studied these women, I did recognize God had purpose in them working. Let's try to unfold and discover the plan, purpose, and the hand of God on these women. There are times, however, in our walk with the Lord that we may never know what the purpose is for a season of our lives until years later. It is even possible that we may never know why we went through a particular season of life. But my hope is to equip you with enough knowledge to make the best decisions for your lives together.

Take some time to study the following scriptures and the stories of the lives of these women.[11] Focus in on what their job was, the reason they were working that particular job, and the season of life they were in as they worked.

- Jochebed: Exodus 2:1-10, Exodus 6:20, Numbers 26:59
- Deborah: Judges 4-5
- Lydia: Acts 16:13-15,40
- Joanna: Luke 24:10, Luke 8:1-3
- Anna: Luke 2:36-38
- Junia: Romans 16:7

Jochebed: (meaning: heavy, honorable, glorious)

- Daughter of Levi.
- Wife of Amram of the house of Levi.
- Mother of Miriam, Aaron, and Moses.
- Allowed Moses to be placed in river by Miriam.
- Pharaoh's daughter took Moses as her own.
- Miriam was sent by Pharaoh's daughter to have Jochebed nurse him.
- Jochebed worked for Pharaoh's daughter nursing Moses (until he was approximately seven years old. Aaron would have been three years old when Moses was born). It is possible that Miriam and Jochebed had great favor at the palace and with Pharaoh's daughter. They most likely lived close to the palace, on palace grounds, or even in servant quarters. They may have done other work for Pharaoh's daughter.

- It is not known if Jochebed lived to see Moses lead the people out of Egypt.

Deborah: (meaning: bee, spirited woman, or woman of fire)

- Israelite women of this era made a substantial contribution to the economy. They planted, weeded, and harvested crops. They processed grain, olives, and fruits for storage.
- Judge of Israel (tribal leader); in times of peace had authority to settle disputes and problems. In times of war acted as a rallying point to gather the tribes and organize resistance.
- Representative of God with messages directly from God.
- Prophetess.
- Summoned Barak (military general); told him what must be done.
- Prophesied honor for a woman (Jael). Jael killed Siersa (the enemy) with a tent peg and a hammer.

Lydia: (meaning: cultured or beauty, from Lydia the region)

- Probably a wealthy business woman; seller of purple cloth (a sign of royalty).
- Heart opened to God.
- Baptized along with her household.
- Worshiper of God.
- Willing servant; opened her home to Paul and companions.
- Active member of the church.

Joanna: (meaning: God is gracious)

- Wife of Chuza.
- Husband's father (Herod the Great) attempted to have Christ killed as an infant.
- Disciple of Christ.
- Discovered empty tomb.
- Healed of various evil spirits and infirmities.
- Most likely supported the work of Christ and disciples financially.

Anna: (means grace)

- Prophetess.
- Tribe of Asher.
- Widow after seven years (married at age twelve).
- Worshiped in temple day and night, fasting and praying.
- Supported by relatives (1 Timothy 5:11-16) and by the church (Acts 6:1, 9:39).
- Confirmed the Christ child.

Junia: (meaning: youthful)

- An apostle.
- Husband thought to be Andronicus.
- Highly regarded by Paul; outstanding among apostles.
- Possibly among 120 mentioned in Acts.
- Fellow prisoner.
- Christian before Paul.
- Possibly one of the founders of church at Rome.

What did you discover about the working women of the Bible? How can you apply this to your current situation or future issues you may face as a wife and mother?

_____

_____

_____

_____

_____

Do you think God has a time and a specific place for where and when you work? In the past have you sought the Lord for direction in regard to working? How has the Lord led you in the past as you pursued a new job or career?

_____

_____

_____

_____

_____

_____

Many issues must be examined if the wife is working outside of the home while raising children. If the husband wants the wife to work, he must be willing to take on greater responsibility. In talking with many young wives, especially those with young children, the majority of them would like to be in the home to raise their children. It would seem it is the husband who is encouraging them to work outside of the home in many instances. We do, however, run into women who truly want to work while raising a family.

The Cadillac of daycare providers cannot give children the exceptional care that a mom and dad can give. Research has proven that the two most important ages for parents to be involved with their children are the preschool years and those years from about eleven to fifteen. It is during these stages that children's conscience and character are developed.

When both mother and father work, it is very important that they assist each other in raising and nurturing the children. It is biblical that we cooperate in marriage roles. Peter says that the husband and wife are heirs together of the grace of life, and Paul says that husbands should treat their wives as Christ does the church. As Christ empowers and elevates the church, husbands should be supportive and partner in the raising of the children as well as the management of the home.[12]

I am not naive to the economic circumstances we live in; however, what I would suggest is seeking the Lord and pondering the following questions.

- Does God have a plan and purpose for you to be working?

_____

_____

- What season of your life are you in?

_____

_____

- If the Lord is leading you into the work force, what field or occupation do you feel led to?

_____

_____

- Who will care for the children?

_____

- Will the children be in a Christian environment?

_____

- Will you work full time or part time?

_____

We Promise

- How much money will you make?
  _____

- How much money will it cost you to work? Such as childcare, gas, vehicle expense, meals out, etc.
  _____

- Will working cause you or your children to miss going to church?
  _____

- What kinds of strain will working put on your marital relationship?
  _____

- If possible, would it be conducive to work at home?
  _____

- Is there an alternative work situation that will make it easier on the family if the wife works?
  _____

- Will the husband working overtime or taking on a second job bring in more money than the wife could by working full time?
  _____

- Will the husband share in the household duties and be willing at times to take on more than the wife?
  _____

If couples will take the time to explore these issues and honestly answer the above questions, they will discover what is best for their family and the season they are in. There may be times in marriage where these issues may need to be revisited.

No one does laundry in fairytales. Young men and woman give little thought about the daily duties of everyday living. Their dreams are far loftier than dishes and garbage. Young men dream about the trophy they will conquer while young girls rehearse their wedding day, not their marriage. The young girl daydreams, looks at magazines, reads romance novels, and wonders who will be her prince. Every date she's on, she wonders, *Is this the one?* She believes in "happily ever afters" and wants no one to wake her up to the realities of life. Engagement comes, and the dream becomes more real to her as she waits for the prince to sweep her off her feet and ride off on his white stallion to their castle. Is this just a dream, or could it be possible that there are truly dreamers whose dreams will be fulfilled? With preparation for those yet to be married and realignment for those already married, dreams can become a reality.

The Bible gives us a picture of the bride (the church) waiting for her groom (Christ Jesus). John 14:1-4 (NKJV) says:

> Let not your heart be troubled; you believe in God, believe also in Me. In My Father's house are many mansions; if *it were not so,* I would have told you. *I go to prepare a place for you. And if I go and prepare a place for you, I will come again and receive you to Myself; that where I am, there you may be also.* And where I go you know, and the way you know.

The groom has gone to prepare a place for His bride. The bride is to make herself ready for the marriage. What an incredible picture we are given in Revelation of the greatest wedding feast to ever take place.

Revelation 19:7-8 (NKJV) says,

> Let us be glad and rejoice and give Him glory, for the marriage of the Lamb has come, *and His wife has made herself ready.*" And to her it was granted to be arrayed in fine linen, clean and bright, for the fine linen is the righteous acts of the saints.

The *groom,* Christ Jesus, comes, and He is on His white horse! Revelation 19:11-17 (NKJV) says,

> Now I saw heaven opened, and behold, a white horse. And He who sat on him *was* called Faithful and True, and in righteousness He judges and makes war. His eyes *were* like a flame of fire, and on His head *were* many crowns.

> He had a name written that no one knew except Himself. He *was* clothed with a robe dipped in blood, and His name is called The Word of God. And the armies in heaven, clothed in fine linen, white and clean, followed Him on white horses. Now out of His mouth goes a sharp sword, that with it He should strike the nations. And He Himself will rule them with a rod of iron. He Himself treads the winepress of the fierceness and wrath of Almighty God. And He has on *His* robe and on His thigh a name written: KING OF KINGS AND LORD OF LORDS. Then I saw an angel standing in the sun; and he cried with a loud voice, saying to all the birds that fly in the midst of heaven, "Come and gather together for the supper of the great God."

Kris Valloton the Senior Associate Leader, founder and overseer of Bethel School of the Supernatural Ministry at Bethel Church in Redding, California writes an introduction in his book titled *The Supernatural Ways of Royalty* that is truly dynamic.

> Perhaps we are better exemplified as the beautiful daughter who will ascend the throne through marriage, for she is betrothed to the Prince of Peace. The Bridal Chamber is being built, the feast is being prepared, and the Bride is making herself ready. Alternatively, we may be called the Children of God, the Engaged Bride, a Royal Priesthood, the Apple of His eye, and a New Creation, but above all, one thing is for certain: We have captivated the heart of our lover. Burning with desire, He has mounted His white horse, assembled a majestic entourage, and is making His way toward the planet![13]

I couldn't have said it better myself. Take notice preparation is made before the marriage takes place. Matthew 22:14 (NIV) says: "For many are invited, but few are chosen." Our desire is to help prepare you as couples to be partakers and reflectors. I believe we as couples could have a taste of heaven on earth reflected in our marriages. If our marriages reflect Jesus Christ and His church, if we would prepare ourselves and adhere to the Bible's way of marriage. The little girl dreams could be fulfilled instead of tarnished, broken, and violated if preparation is made. We realize we still live in a sin-filled world, but we have a choice to step into the roles God has called us to and, by His mercy and grace, fulfill those godly roles and be a radiant reflection of Jesus and His bride. It is never too late; even if you've been married for years, the Lord is in the restoration business, and He will give you what you need to change bad habits into good ones and realign your heart to follow!

I remember when my oldest daughter was engaged. One evening her fiancé was coming to pick her up. She had literally primped for hours making herself ready for their date. As time approached for him to arrive, she ran down the stairs looking out the window, saying, "Is he here yet?" Then she ran back up the stairs to primp a little more. She was giddy with excitement for her love to come. When he did arrive, her eyes gleamed with joy that was unexplainable. She ran back up the stairs to allow me to answer the door so when she came down the open staircase, he would have full view of her. Their eyes locked upon each other, and nothing could distract them. After they left for their date, the Lord impressed upon my heart that is how I should be as I await King Jesus to come and sweep me off my feet for the marriage supper of the Lamb. I felt extremely disappointed in myself; when I was awakened to the longing Jesus has for His bride to anticipate Him, I had fallen very short.

    I challenge us as women to spend as much time preparing our hearts as we do preparing our outside package. 1 Peter 3:3-5 (NKJV) says:

> Do not let your adornment be *merely* outward—arranging the hair, wearing gold, or putting on *fine* apparel—rather *let it be* the hidden person of the heart, with the incorruptible *beauty* of a gentle and quiet spirit, which is very precious in the sight of God. For in this manner, in former times, the holy women who trusted in God also adorned themselves, being submissive to their own husbands.

Are you ready, ladies? It's time to define your role as a wife.

Foundational Stone Four

> There's no one like her on earth, never has been, never will be. She's a woman beyond compare. My dove is perfection, Pure and innocent as the day she was born.
>
> Song of Solomon 6:8-9 (MSG)

In your own words write: *My role as a wife is*:

_____

_____

_____

_____

_____

_____

_____

_____

> I am my lover's, and he claims me as his own.
>
> Song of Solomon 7:10 (NLT)

Honor Guards

> Marriage is honorable among all, and the bed undefiled; but fornicators and adulterers God will judge.
>
> Hebrews 13:4 (NKJV)

> Above all else, guard your heart, for it is the wellspring of life.
>
> Proverbs 4:23 (NIV)

In this chapter titled "Honor Guards," we will cover three separate foundational stones. These foundational stones will deal with honoring and safeguarding your relationship. Honoring someone may have several facets involved when it comes to relationships. Safeguarding your relationship may also curtail many principles. For the sake of this study, it would be difficult to separate honoring and guarding principles. The two go hand in hand when it comes to marriage.

When I think of *honor*, words that come to my mind are:

- reverence
- respect
- acknowledgement
- admiration
- worthiness
- acceptance
- esteem
- attention

- loyalty
- trustworthiness
- forgiving
- purity

The Greek meaning of the word *honor*[14] is: "valuable, costly, esteemed, beloved, dear, and precious."

The Bible has examples of honor that are worthy of study. Let's take a look at a few of these examples. Look up the following passages and fill in the blanks.

Genesis 14:17-24: How did Abram honor Melchizedek?

_____

_____

1 Chronicles 21:20-28: How did David honor the Lord and honor Araunah?

_____

_____

Esther: How did Esther honor her God, her people, and Mordecai?

_____

_____

2 Kings 2:1-14: How did Elisha honor Elijah?

_____

_____

We Promise

Genesis 29:16-30: How did Jacob honor Rachel?

_____

_____

Ruth 1:11-18: How did Ruth honor Naomi?

_____

_____

Romans 16:1-16: Paul made mention of many servants of the Lord; how did he honor them? Who do you think stands out amongst this roll call?

_____

_____

Years ago we had the privilege of becoming friends with Eric and Colleen. Our friendship was easily developed because we shared much in common. Our beliefs in God are the same as well as our love for the water. We are all *bona fide* Lakers to the fullest extent. As we grew to know Eric and Colleen, it became very evident that their love for each other was deeply rooted, and they were true examples of honoring one another. Their love story is well worth sharing.

Eric and Colleen were high school sweethearts. Being each other's best friends and truly loving one another, they married young and together had one son. Summer as well as winter activities have always been paramount in their lives. They have been very active physically. Eric and Colleen are the type of people who live life to the fullest and are diligent to see any task as well as activity through. They have now been married for forty years.

About fifteen years ago after returning from a downhill skiing trip to Utah, Colleen had a severe stroke. Life as they knew it changed dynamically. Even though Colleen is a determined, strong woman, the best of medicine and rehabilitation could not reverse the damage of the stroke or grant her a full recovery. The last few years have brought on increased medical challenges with many hospitalizations. One thing that has always been evident to Dan and me is Eric's undying devotion and support of Colleen. Eric always honors his wife in word and deed; when he speaks of her, he says she is unstoppable, his love for her is undying, and he calls her his bride. Together they have faced great challenges, especially these last few years.

Colleen fights for victory over the physical challenges she faces and Eric does whatever he can to keep life as they knew it. Eric has maintained an incredible attitude. He always has a smile on his face, remaining upbeat and hopeful. He never once has expressed to us frustration or complained about their situation. He admires Colleen's steadfast determination to keep on going, despite each day's challenge. Through hospital and rehabilitation stays, Eric has remained by his bride's side, encouraging and spurring her on. It is very common for him to spend the night with her at these facilities. Together they have faced challenges with great tenacity and determination to overcome and keep on going.

The traditions that they established in their younger years have continued to this day. From the simplest details of decorating for the holidays to remodeling their house and saving time for the water, unrelenting passions and a love for their God has kept them going. Dan and I have often discussed how difficult these last fifteen years must have been for them as a couple; we are convinced they are a true example of honoring one another.

Eric and Colleen are a delightful couple. Any young couple would be wise to latch onto a couple such as Eric and Colleen and learn what honor and love really is. We highly recommend young couples find an older seasoned couple who is rooted in God and be mentored by them. Dan and I are advocates of marriage mentoring and oversee a marriage mentor program at our church. The young couples who participate in this program really love it and have benefited greatly from the relationship they have formed with their marriage mentors.

We are to honor in thought, word, and deed. Making our thoughts pure is of the utmost importance, because when the pressure, tension, conflict, and emergencies occur, what we have dwelt on in thought will surely manifest verbally. The Bible has much to say about our thoughts. Study the following scriptures.

> Casting down arguments and every high thing that exalts itself against the knowledge of God, bringing every thought into captivity to the obedience of Christ.
>
> 2 Corinthians 10:5 (NKJV)

> Finally, brethren, whatever things are true, whatever things are noble, whatever things are just, whatever things are pure, whatever things are lovely, whatever things are of good report, if there is any virtue and if there is anything praiseworthy; meditate on these things.
>
> Philippians 4:8 (NKJV)

Brood of vipers! How can you, being evil, speak good things? *For out of the abundance of the heart the mouth speaks.* A good man out of the good treasure of his heart brings forth good things, and an evil man out of the evil treasure brings forth evil things. But I say to you that for every idle word men may speak, they will give account of it in the day of judgment. For by your words you will be justified, and by your words you will be condemned.

Matthew 12:34 (NKJV)

We must choose our words wisely, being determined to always speak words that will build up and never tear down. Your words and deeds must align with one another if you are going to truly edify your partner. Study the following scriptures in regard to the words we speak and the actions which must follow.

> *Death and life are in the power of the tongue*, and those who love it will eat its fruit.
>
> Proverbs 18:21 (NKJV)

> *Keep your tongue from evil,* And your *lips from speaking deceit. Depart from evil and do good; seek peace and pursue it.* The eyes of the Lord are on the righteous, and His ears are open to their cry. The face of the Lord is against those who do evil, to cut off the remembrance of them from the earth. The righteous cry out, and the Lord hears, and delivers them out of all their troubles.
>
> Psalm 34:13-17 (NKJV)

> Therefore *let us pursue the things which make for peace and the things by which one may edify another.*
>
> Romans 14:19 (NKJV)

> Let each of us *please his neighbor for his good, leading to edification.*
>
> Romans 15:2 (NKJV)

> Therefore *receive one another,* just as Christ also received us, to the glory of God.
>
> Romans 15:7 (NKJV)

But let us who are of the day be sober, putting on the breastplate of faith and love, and as a helmet the hope of salvation. For God did not appoint us to wrath, but to obtain salvation through our Lord Jesus Christ, who died for us, that whether we wake or sleep, we should live together with Him. Therefore *comfort each other and edify one another*, just as you also are doing. And we urge you, brethren, to *recognize those who labor among you*, and are over you in the Lord and admonish you, and to *esteem them very highly in love f*or their work's sake. *Be at peace among yourselves.* Now we exhort you, brethren, warn those who are unruly, *comfort the fainthearted, uphold the weak, be patient with all.* See *that no one renders evil for evil to anyone*, but *always pursue what is good both for yourselves and for all.* Rejoice always, pray without ceasing.

1 Thessalonians 5:8-17 (NKJV)

But *exhort one another daily*, while it is called "Today," lest any of you be hardened through the deceitfulness of sin.

Hebrews 3:13 (NKJV)

Not returning evil for evil or reviling for reviling, but on the contrary blessing, knowing that you were called to this, that you may inherit a blessing. For "He who would love life and see good days, let him *refrain his tongue from evil*, and his *lips from speaking deceit.* Let him *turn away from evil and do good; let him seek peace and pursue it.* For the eyes of the LORD are on the righteous, and His ears are open to their prayers; But the face of the LORD is against those who do evil." And who is he who will harm you if you become followers of what is good? But even if you should suffer for righteousness' sake, you are blessed. "And do not be afraid of their threats, nor be troubled." But sanctify the Lord God in your hearts, and always be ready to give a defense to everyone who asks you a reason for the hope that is in you, with meekness and fear; having a good conscience, that when they defame you as evildoers, those who revile your good conduct in Christ may be ashamed. *For it is better, if it is the will of God, to suffer for doing good than for doing evil.*

1 Peter 3:9-17 (NKJV)

But the end of all things is at hand; therefore *be serious and watchful in your prayers.* And above all things *have fervent love for one another*, for "love will cover a multitude of sins." *Be hospitable to one another without grumbling.* As each one has received a gift, *minister it to one another*, as good stewards of the manifold grace of God. If anyone speaks, *let him speak as the oracles of God.* If anyone ministers, let him do it as with the ability which God supplies, that in all things God may be glorified through Jesus Christ, to whom belong the glory and the dominion forever and ever. Amen.

1 Peter 4:7-11 (NKJV)

I beseech you therefore, brethren, by the mercies of God, that you present your bodies a living sacrifice, holy, acceptable to God, which is your reasonable service. And do not be conformed to this world, but *be transformed by the renewing of your mind*, that you may prove what is that good and acceptable and perfect will of God.

Romans 12:1-2 (NKJV)

Do not be deceived, God is not mocked; for whatever a man sows, that he will also reap. For he who sows to his flesh will of the flesh reap corruption, but he who sows to the Spirit will of the Spirit reap everlasting life. And *let us not grow weary while doing good*, for in due season we shall reap if we do not lose heart. Therefore, as we have opportunity, *let us do good to all*, especially to those who are of the household of faith.

Galatians 6:7-10 (NKJV)

Continue earnestly in prayer, being vigilant in it with thanksgiving.

Colossians 4:2 (NKJV)

Walk in wisdom toward those who are outside, redeeming the time. Let your speech always be with grace, seasoned with salt, that you may know how you ought to answer each one.

Colossians 4:5-6 (NKJV)

So then, my beloved brethren, let every man be swift to hear, slow to speak, slow to wrath; for the wrath of man does not produce the righteousness of God. Therefore lay aside all filthiness and overflow of wickedness, and receive with meekness the implanted word, which is able to save your souls. *But be doers of the word, and not hearers only*, deceiving yourselves.

James 1:19-22 (NKJV)

Look up and read: Romans 12:9-20

In his book, *Love Life for Every Married Couple*,[15] Dr. Ed Wheat encourages the reader to put every thought, word, or deed to a test. He suggests we utilize and answer the following questions when issues arise. Dr. Ed. Wheat has decades of experience as a family physician and certified sex therapist. He along with his wife, Gloria, has written numerous books on subjects pertaining to marriage.

- Will this bring us closer or drive us apart?
- Will it lift up or tear down our relationship?
- Will it cause a positive response or a negative response?
- Does it express my love and loyalty to my spouse, or does it reveal my selfishness?

I mentioned earlier that honoring and guarding go hand in hand. When we honor our spouse, we are going to put safeguards in place to protect our relationship. We are also going to put safeguards in place with relationships outside of marriage to protect our marriage from outside invasion. Each of us knows ourselves, our strengths and weaknesses. We know how weak we are to fall prey to certain situations, places, or people. Do not set yourself up for failure, but set yourself up for success. A recovering alcoholic protects themselves from places and people that would cause them to fall off the wagon. Hence, it would be very unwise for a recovering alcoholic to go to a bar to watch the football game and socialize with those who are drinking (Do not be misled: "Bad company corrupts good character," 1 Corinthians 15:33, NIV). The whole point is to keep boundaries around you and under no circumstance cross them.

Today, due to movies, TV, and media, we have grown numb to what healthy relationships are and how to conduct ourselves in relationships outside of the marriage. The Bible commands us to leave the most intimate of relationships (that of the father and mother) and cleave unto our spouse, becoming one. If we are commanded to leave this most intimate relationship, how much more should this apply to relationships or friendships that distract from our marital commitment? Please make no mistake; we are not saying you cannot have friends, we are saying when those relationships take away from your marriage, stealing time or invading privacy, they must be re-evaluated. A growing trend among young people today is best friends of the opposite sex. Should this type of relationship continue after one marries, it may sabotage your marriage. Coworkers can also be an issue when it comes to the martial relationship. You have heard the saying "misery likes company." It's true. Unfortunately a lot of complaining about one's spouse goes on in the workplace. Run from such talk, or you will find yourself joining in on the complaint party and becoming dissatisfied with your spouse.

The following are some basic questions to answer that will help aid you in developing safeguards for your relationship. This list is not all inclusive. You know your own weaknesses; add or delete from this list to help you form safeguards for your relationship.

We Promise

- If you share private issues with someone other than your spouse, how will this affect your relationship?

  _____

  _____

- What could occur if you shared with someone what your spouse has told you in confidence?

  _____

  _____

- If you speak poorly of your spouse to your parents, what will begin to occur?

  _____

  _____

- Calling your parents to discuss a fight you had with your spouse may have some negative ramifications. What would some of these ramifications be?

  _____

  _____

- What things in your home could affect your relationship negatively?

  _____

  _____

  _____

- Should you ever be alone with the opposite sex?

   _____

   _____

- Chitchatting on the phone, e-mails, or Facebooking with the opposite sex could cause what to take place in your relationship with your spouse?

   _____

   _____

- Flirting with the opposite sex will have what type of an effect on your relationship?

   _____

   _____

- What should you do if you find yourself thinking about someone of the opposite sex?

   _____

   _____

- What happens when we do not really listen to our spouse and jump to conclusions?

   _____

   _____

- What safeguards should be put in place with coworkers of the opposite sex?

   _____

We Promise

- When taking breaks at work, what are some ways you can safeguard your marital relationship?

  _____

  _____

- Should you ever go to a party or out after work with members of the opposite sex? How could this affect your relationship?

  _____

  _____

- What will happen if you do not tell your spouse where you are at all times?

  _____

  _____

- If it is possible, do you always answer phone calls from your spouse immediately?

  _____

  _____

- Do I respect my spouse when calling them if they are at work or in a meeting?

  _____

  _____

- Does my spouse get my undivided attention when he or she is talking to me? Do I look him or her in the eye? Do I clarify that I understand what he or she is trying to relay to me?

  _____

  _____

- Whom should I flirt with on a daily basis? What are some ways I can flirt with my spouse?

  _____

  _____

- When referring to my spouse in conversations with others, how should I speak of my spouse?

  _____

  _____

- Am I willing to lay aside my agenda to serve my spouse? In what ways can I do this?

  _____

  _____

- Are date nights important to me? What are some ways I can bring more meaning to date nights?

  _____

  _____

We Promise

- How does my relationship with the Lord affect my relationship with my spouse? What are some changes I can make that will bring about positive results?

  _____

  _____

- What types of control should be put on the Internet to protect our marriage, including e-mail, Facebook, etc.?

  _____

  _____

- What types of guidelines should be placed on TV, movies, and books?

  _____

  _____

- How should our thought life be controlled?

  _____

  _____

- When traveling to work or other destinations, should I ever be alone in a car with the opposite sex? How could this affect my marriage?

  _____

  _____

- Does my spouse have the freedom to check on my activities via the computer, including e-mails?

- What value would an accountability partner be in areas of my life where I have weaknesses?

- Do you have a spiritual mentor? If not, is there an older, more mature believer you could ask?

- How will my relationship be impacted if I always remember: birthdays, anniversaries, Valentine's Day, etc.?

- What can I do to reduce the stress load of my spouse?

We Promise

- How can I be proactive and look for ways to bless my spouse in words, thoughts, and deeds?

  _____

  _____

- How can I get to know my spouse better?

  _____

  _____

- What will happen if I keep secrets from my spouse? How can I prevent this from happening?

  _____

  _____

- List some ways you can study your spouse and get to know them better. What are some questions you can ask that will let them know you are truly interested in their desires and dreams?

  _____

  _____

  _____

  _____

Foundational Stone Five

> But Ruth said: "Entreat me not to leave you, Or to turn back from following after you; For wherever you go, I will go; And wherever you lodge, I will lodge; Your people shall be my people, And your God, my God. Where you die, I will die, And there will I be buried. The LORD do so to me, and more also, If anything but death parts you and me."
>
> Ruth 1:16-17 (NKJV)

In your own words define: *I will honor my wife in the following ways:*

_____

_____

_____

_____

_____

_____

_____

_____

Foundational Stone Six

In your own words define: *I will honor my husband in the following ways:*

_____

_____

_____

_____

_____

_____

_____

_____

_____

_____

Foundational Stone Seven

As a couple, write out in your own words: *We will safeguard our marital relationship by placing these boundaries around personal habits and relationships outside of marriage:*

_____

_____

_____

_____

_____

_____

_____

_____

_____

But the Lord is faithful, who will establish you and guard you from the evil one.
2 Thessalonians 3:3 (NKJV)

Ours for the Keeping: Sex and Intimacy

My lover is mine, and I am his. Nightly he strolls in our garden, delighting in the flowers until dawn breathes its light and night slips away.
>					Song of Solomon 2:16 (MSG)

But my vineyard is all mine, and I'm keeping it to myself.
>					Song of Solomon 8:11 (MSG)

There are two things that rank way up there on a scale of one to ten that are *almost* as good as sex. Water skiing on a hot, sunny, calm day, and watching the fireworks from our waterfront cottage on the Fourth of July (fireworks over the Cinderella castle at Disney ranks way up there also), and yes, you got it, a woman is writing this. After a fantastic water ski run, it is not unusual for me to climb in the boat and exclaim to my husband, "That was almost as good as sex!" I have also been known to yell that out while skiing, realizing no one could hear me above the boat motor. I would not be able to say this if we had not protected and valued our sexual relationship as a couple.

If you want the greatest sexual experience, intimacy must be a partner. I have owned and operated an educational training service for many years. One of the services I teach is CPR and AED to medical and lay professionals. Since AEDs have come on the scene, more and more lives have been saved. CPR and AED work together. The greatest survival rate is when the two are used efficiently together. CPR sustains the life while the AED shocks the heart into a normal beating pattern; together a life can be saved. If you did nothing until the AED arrived, the chance of survival would be grim. Likewise, if you only performed CPR without the intervention of the AED, survival once again would be grim. Sex without intimacy will die and become a meaningless act; however, intimacy coupled with sex will produce life-giving closeness which is yours for the keeping. This type of closeness creates an incredible desire for one another such as is written in the Song of Solomon. We highly recommend you read the Song of Solomon out of *The Message*.

A lifetime of marriage can throw all kinds of issues, obstacles, events, emergencies, lows, and highs our way. One great benefit of marriage is that our sexual relationship can be a steadfast warmth of enjoyment and shelter from life's storms regardless of what else we may face. The greatest comfort at the end of a long, busy, hard day can be climbing into bed and lying next to your love in the safety and warmth of their arms. After you have shared a time of peaceful comfort, partaking of the lovely gift of the sexual union is extremely fulfilling. I realize that there can be issues where due to medical reasons, alterations to the sexual relationship may transpire. Please notice I said *alterations*; if you are facing medical issues that have affected your sexual relationship, seeking professional counseling will be of great benefit to you.

There are safeguards and good habits we can put in place that will enable our relationships to flourish when it comes to sex and intimacy. The Bible says we will reap what we sow, and that can be applied to this area of marriage. Sexual purity before and after marriage is paramount to your marital relationship. When a cement foundation is poured, rebar is placed strategically throughout for strength, stability, and to limit cracking. The rebar is in place before the cement is poured. Sexual purity is the rebar of the sexual relationship. We will need to spend some time now learning about sexual purity and its importance before and after marriage. The word pure comes out of a Greek word *hagnos* or *aminantos*,[16] which means to be free from all taint which is lewd. Repentance and forgiveness will be of great importance as well when it comes to the sexual relationship; however, this will be elaborated on later in this manual.

First off, we must be willing to call sin, sin. Sexual impurity is sin. The Lord created within us a sex drive, but with the drive He gave us the responsibility to use it within His guidelines. This passion or drive must be fulfilled with God's purpose for us. The Bible has much to say about sex. Sex goes beyond the physical; it also entails the thought life; keep this in mind while studying the following verses and writings.

> For this *is the will of God*, your sanctification: that you *should abstain from sexual immorality*; that each of you should know how to possess his own vessel in sanctification and honor, *not in passion of lust*, like the Gentiles who do not know God; that no one should take advantage of and defraud his

We Promise

> brother in this matter, because the Lord *is* the avenger of all such, as we also forewarned you and testified. For God did not call us to uncleanness, but in holiness. Therefore *he who rejects this does not reject man, but God*, who has also given us His Holy Spirit.
>
> 1 Thessalonians 4:3-8 (NKJV)

According to 1 Thessalonians 4:3-8, answer the following questions in your own words:

- What is the will of God?

  _____

- What are we to abstain from?

  _____

- How are we to possess our vessel?

  _____

- What do you think sanctification and honor are? (You may want to look these words up in the dictionary.)

  _____

  _____

  _____

- What is passion of lust?

  _____

- What would you consider taking advantage of or defrauding a brother/sister means?

  _____

- Whom do we reject when we are sexually immoral?

  _____

- How would you describe sexual immorality?

  _____

- List some acts, thoughts, or deeds that you consider sexually impure:

  _____

  _____

Clearly, the Bible has said this is the will of God; there is no mistake. We are to abstain from sexual immorality. The act of remaining pure means refraining from and avoiding all actions and excitements that are sexual and not within the safety net of the marriage union. This relationship (marriage union) is defined between one man and woman for a lifetime. The passion and excitement of the sexual aspects in thought, word, and deed is reserved solely for the husband and wife, to be shared with no other persons.

In Leviticus 18, laws were given in regard to sex. The words *sexual relations*[17] used throughout this chapter come from the Hebrew phrase that literally means "uncover the nakedness of" (the uncovering of nakedness) a person who is not your lawful wife or husband. The fact is, 1 Corinthians 6:18 (NKJV) states: "Flee sexual immorality. Every sin that a man does is outside the body, but he who commits sexual immorality sins against his own body." According to *Strong's Concordance*, to flee sexual immorality[18] means: "to run away, vanish, escape, shun anything that would cause you to indulge in unlawful lust." Unlawful is referring to someone who is not your spouse. The word *lust*,[19] according to *Webster's Dictionary*, means "intense sexual desire; an intense longing; a craving." When we consider in Leviticus that sexual relations is the uncovering of nakedness, we can then read in Matthew that Jesus took this even further to say, "But I say to you that whoever *looks at a woman to lust for her has already committed adultery with her in his heart*" (Matthew 5:28, NKJV).

Of course, this is also applicable to the woman who would lust after a man. Pondering these verses, we must realize sexual impurity encompasses our whole being of thought, word, and deed. Before you commit a deed or act, the thought has crossed your mind first, and this is the place you must seize if you're going to remain sexually pure before and after marriage.

We Promise

Read Genesis 39:2-12. How did Joseph overcome temptation? In verse 9, what does Joseph say in regard to whom he was sinning against, and what did he call this potential sin?

_____

_____

_____

When the Bible says if you commit sexual immorality you sin against your own body, what do you think this means? What ramifications do you think can occur when you sin against your own body?

_____

_____

_____

Do you think there are consequences to sin? What are some consequences that could occur if you have sex outside of marriage?

_____

_____

_____

As believers, we are to live according to the Word of God, and a challenge is placed before us in 2 Corinthians.

> Therefore, *Come out from among them And be separate*, says the Lord. Do not touch what is unclean, And I will receive you. I will be a Father to you, And

you shall be My sons and daughters, Says the Lord Almighty. Therefore, having these promises, beloved, let us cleanse ourselves from all filthiness of the flesh and spirit, perfecting holiness in the fear of God.

2 Corinthians 6:17-7:1 (NKJV)

What safeguards can we put in place that will enable us to be separate from the ways of the world and unbelievers when it comes to sexuality?

_____

What will happen if we touch what is unclean?

_____

As pastoral biblical counselors, we are constantly faced with counseling young couples who are professing to be Christians who are living together. We encourage these couples to make separate living arrangements along with a pledge to purity until marriage. It is not unusual for these couples to tell us, "We are just living together, not having sex." They will also proclaim the Bible does not say you cannot live together; this is a growing epidemic among believers. When a couple tries to convince us they are living together but not having sex, we like to read the following passage to them. It is the story about the woman at the well (John 4:4-42, NKJV).

For the sake of addressing this issue of living together (co-habitating), let's dig a little further into each of these verses taken from John 4:4-42 (NKJV) and explore the history of the times to reap greater meaning and relevance on the subject.

- "It was about the sixth hour." The sixth hour is of significance due to the fact most women would have walked this approximately two miles early in the morning. The younger women would have been the ones to draw and carry the water. Most likely the Samaritan woman came at the sixth hour to avoid stares and ridicule from the other women. She knew she would be shunned due to her lifestyle. Jesus planned on being there to have an encounter with this woman. This was not a chance meeting, for many would be saved as a result of this encounter. John 4:4 (NKJV) states, "But He needed to go through Samaria." A Jew would not normally travel through Samaria. The Jews shunned the Samaritans because of their mixed beliefs of Judaism and pagan religion.

- "And He would have given you living water." Jesus had a gift for this woman that would bring to her life and freedom. This gift would liberate her from a life of sin and bondage into a life of healing and renewal. Jesus says if we drink the water He gives, we will never thirst again and His water is a spring, giving eternal life.

- "I have no husband." Jesus said to her, "You have well said, 'I have no husband,' for you have had five husbands, and the one whom you now have is not your husband; in that you spoke truly." (John 4:17-18, NKJV) Jesus, using a Word of knowledge, identifies this woman has had five husbands, and the one she lived with now was not her husband (several Bible translations use the words "the one she lived with"). This is very interesting that Jesus does not say, "The one she is committing adultery or fornication with." He says, "The one you are living with now." I am not a theologian and certainly would never want to take a scripture out of context. Why didn't Jesus say the one you are committing adultery or fornication with (having unlawful sexual immorality)? I am uncertain how to answer that question, but one thing I do know is Jesus did identify the fact that the man she was living with was not her husband. Jesus was offering her a new life, a way of escape from her former way of living.

- "For the Father is seeking such to worship Him." Samaritans mixed Judaism with pagan practices (occult). Jesus wanted this woman to know who He was and whom she should be worshiping. "I who speak to you am He." In John 14:16 (NKJV) the Bible says, "Jesus said to him, 'I am the way, the truth, and the life. No one comes to the Father except through Me.'"

- "The woman then left her water pot, went her way into the city, and said to the men, "Come, see a Man who told me all things that I ever did. Could this be the Christ?" This Samaritan woman acknowledged that Jesus knew all the things she had ever done. Because of this knowledge she wondered, *Could this be the Christ?* (John 4:27, NKJV) Who else could have known everything she had ever done? The Bible tells us in the following verses that sin is always disclosed.

  - 1 Corinthians 14:25 (NKJV), "And thus the secrets of his heart are revealed; and so, falling down on his face, he will worship God and report that God is truly among you."

  - Matthew 10:26 (NKJV), "Therefore do not fear them. For there is nothing covered that will not be revealed, and hidden that will not be known."

  - Mark 4:22 (NKJV), "For there is nothing hidden which will not be revealed, nor has anything been kept secret but that it should come to light."

- Luke 8:17 (NKJV), "For nothing is secret that will not be revealed, nor *anything* hidden that will not be known and come to light."
- Luke 12:2 (NKJV), "For there is nothing covered that will not be revealed, nor hidden that will not be known."
- Ezekiel 21:24 (NKJV), "Therefore thus says the Lord GOD: 'Because you have made your iniquity to be remembered, in that your transgressions are uncovered, so that in all your doings your sins appear—because you have come to remembrance, you shall be taken in hand'."

- "My food is to do the will of Him who sent Me, and to finish His work." (John 4:34, NKJV) Jesus was revealing the will of the Father and doing what the Father wanted Him to do. Jesus was seeking out the lost to bring them to salvation.
- "And many of the Samaritans of that city believed in Him because of the word of the woman who testified, 'He told me all that I ever did'" (John 4:39, NKJV). The Samaritans believed and Jesus fulfilled the will of the Father, which was to seek and save those who were lost. "For the Son of Man has come to seek and to save that which was lost" (Luke 19:10, NKJV). "Then they said to the woman, 'Now we believe, not because of what you said, for we ourselves have heard Him and we know that this is indeed the Christ, the Savior of the world'" (John 4:42, NKJV).

Jesus knew this Samaritan woman and that the life she was living would not lead to eternal life. He wanted to give her something that would truly satisfy and fill her void, restoring her to be a true worshiper of God. Through the testimony of this Samaritan woman many came to salvation. The following questions are for those who are living together to answer. If this does not apply to you, skip these questions.

How did you meet?

_____

_____

_____

We Promise

When did you move in together?

_____

Why did you move in together?

_____

_____

_____

How is your relationship with your parents?

_____

_____

How do your parents feel about your living together?

_____

_____

_____

Even though you say you are not having sexual relations (if applicable), since you live together, the unsaved world will not believe you are refraining from sex. What testimony does this portray to the unsaved world?

_____

_____

We are called to come out from among them. To live in this world but not be a part of this world and the way they live. Do you feel you are hurting your Christian testimony? Do you feel you may cause a weaker Christian to stumble and fall?

_____

_____

_____

How does this effect family and friends, and does it jeopardize your relationship with them?

_____

_____

_____

What will you say to your future children when they find out you lived together prior to marriage?

_____

_____

_____

Would you want your daughter or son living with the opposite sex prior to marriage? In regard to your own children one day, do you think this would give security and stability to their life if they lived with someone outside of marriage?

We Promise

Read Ephesians 5:3-5 (NIV) and fill in the blanks.

But among you there must _____, or of any kind of _____, or of _____, because these are improper for God's holy people. Nor should there be _____, _____, or course _____, which are out of place, but rather thanksgiving. Or of this you can be sure: No _____, _____ or greedy person _____.

Do you think you can profess to be a Christian and be living in sexual sin?

_____

How much immoral behavior or impure talk is acceptable?

_____

According to Galatians 5:19-25, what are the works of the flesh?

1. _____
2. _____
3. _____
4. _____
5. _____
6. _____
7. _____
8. _____
9. _____
10. _____
11. _____
12. _____
13. _____
14. _____
15. _____
16. _____
17. _____

If we practice these things, what will happen?

_____

_____

_____

_____

What are the fruits of the Spirit?

1. _____
2. _____
3. _____
4. _____
5. _____
6. _____
7. _____
8. _____
9. _____

What do you think the works of the flesh and the fruits of the Spirit have to do with sexuality purity?

_____

_____

_____

_____

We Promise

According to 1 Thessalonians 4:4, each of us is to control our own body. We need to study ourselves and know our weaknesses and strengths. We should be aware of what entices us and avoid it at all costs. We should know what encourages us to purity and chase after that, wearing it like a garment.

How can you control your own body?

_____

_____

_____

What specific places, people, situations, or activities will you need to avoid so you do not fall into sexual impurity?

_____

_____

_____

What types of activities will promote healthy lifestyle living when it comes to sexual purity?

_____

_____

_____

_____

Are there any items in your home, office, or car that could lure you into sexual sin? If so, how can you change these environments to edify purity of life?

_____

_____

_____

You have heard it said that the eyes are the window to the soul. In an indirect way that saying was taken from the Bible.

> The lamp of the body is the eye. If therefore your eye is good, your whole body will be full of light.
>
> Matthew 6:22 (NKJV)

> I have made a covenant with my eyes; Why then should I look upon a young woman?
>
> Job 31:1 (NKJV)

> Turn away my eyes from looking at worthless things, *and* revive me in Your way.
>
> Psalm 119:37 (NKJV)

> The eyes of your understanding being enlightened; that you may know what is the hope of His calling, what are the riches of the glory of His inheritance in the saints.
>
> Ephesians 1:18 (NKJV)

What we allow in through our eyes will eventually permeate our soul. Most people do not jump into full-blown sin. It sneaks in a little at a time until it snares us completely. Genesis 4:7 (NKJV) says, "If you do well, will you not be accepted? *And if you do not do well, sin lies at the door. And its desire is for you,* but you should rule over it." When we possess self-control, we can withstand and resist sin. 1 Peter 5:8-10 (NKJV) says:

> Be sober, be vigilant; because your adversary the devil walks about like a roaring lion, seeking whom he may devour. *Resist him, steadfast in the faith,* knowing that the same sufferings are experienced by your brotherhood in the world. But may the God of all grace, who called us to His eternal glory by Christ Jesus, after you have suffered a while, perfect, establish, strengthen, and settle *you.*

Pornography is introduced through the eyes, but it doesn't stay there. The destructive forces of pornography shatter relationships on a daily basis, and its desire is never satisfied. Look up and read 2 Peter 2:11-22. In verse 14 notice what is said about the eyes and what is not satisfied. "*They commit adultery with their eyes, and their desire for sin is never satisfied.* They lure unstable people into sin, and they are well trained in greed. *They live under God's curse*" (2 Peter 2:14, NLT). We are reminded in Psalms, "I will set before my eyes no vile thing. The deeds of faithless men I hate; they will not cling to me" (Psalm 101:3, NIV). Believers must take this growing trend for pornography very seriously and move forward, making steps to reverse this tragic problem before more marriages and families are destroyed. H.B. London Jr. is the Vice President of Ministry Outreach/Pastoral Ministries at Focus on the Family. He has written numerous books and hosts a daily radio program. H. B. London Jr. has alluded to the following in an article[20] he wrote:

> Sexual addiction is a major problem in the ministry. At Focus on the Family, we surmise that more than one in five pastors have a problem in the area of pornography. Research in *The Sexual Man* shows that 15.5 percent of married men who are not clergy and 6.8 percent of married clergy continue to masturbate to pornography. Why? From his research, Dr. Hart concludes that sex has become dehumanized. In many circles, it is no longer regarded as an act between loving, responsible couples. Sex has become a sport. And, as in all sports, there is a strong desire to improve one's performance — pornography is a tool. Ministers are not excluded from this game.

If you are involved in pornography, we suggest you get professional counsel now. If you are not married, postpone marriage until you are set free from this ensnaring addiction. This problem will not be solved by marriage. The following websites may give you some insight on how to be set free from the vice of pornography: http://www.pureintimacy.org, http://www.settingcaptivesfree.com.

According the following scriptures, how can you protect yourself from sexual impurity? Proverbs 4:20-27; 5: 7-8,15-18; 6:23-24; 7:7, 22-23; Romans 13:14; Philippians 4:8; Romans 12:1-2; 2 Timothy 2:22; 1 Corinthians 10:13; 1 Peter 1:13-15.

_____

_____

_____

_____

_____

_____

Developing sexual intimacy not only leads to a great sex life, it also adds great stability in remaining pure for the married couple. I cannot think of a greater way of developing intimacy than that of studying your spouse. Know what makes them tick; their likes, dislikes, hopes, fears, as well as dreams. Becoming an A+ student of your spouse will yield incredible dividends for years to come. This is one subject that does not end after a semester; it is a lifelong learning technique. Each of us as individuals is very unique and ever changing. We hear couples say all the time, "My spouse changed. They're not like they were when we first married." Yes, we are in a constant state of transformation and hopefully for the better. If we are seeking the Lord and striving for maturity as a believer, the Bible assures us, "But we all, with unveiled face, beholding as in a mirror the glory of the Lord, *are being transformed into the same image from glory to glory*, just as by the Spirit of the Lord" (2 Corinthians 3:18, NKJV).

Dan and I are certainly much different than when we were first married, praise the Lord! I cannot imagine making it through over thirty years of marriage without the changes that have taken place in us individually and as a couple. When we were first married, we were very self-centered, wanting our own way. As we grew and matured in the Lord and in years, we learned about dying to self and putting other's needs above our own. We also learned when you bless your spouse it is contagious; you receive blessing back.

One of the best things we ever did for our marriage, which led to greater intimacy, was we started taking walks each night for about an hour. Occasionally we would take our children, but most of the time we reserved this time for us. During this hour we could share our day, our hopes, our dreams, and our fears and discuss any issues about the children that needed attention. Growing together caused us to let go of some of our individual activities and find ones we both liked or involved the whole family. We became each other's best friends to the extent that we would rather be with each other than anyone else. Times out with the boys or the girls were less important and infrequent.

As a family, boating was one of our favorite activities. We became *bona fide* lakers, tubing and skiing our way through the summer. As a couple we are very active and enjoy water skiing, kayaking, paddle boating, pontooning, bicycling, walks, and cross-country skiing in the winter. Often we have discussed how thankful we are that we developed this friendship and being active together, because we have noticed other couples our age do not have the enthusiasm we do for activities. Now, do not get me wrong, occasionally I will go for coffee with a friend, but that is rare. We do enjoy getting together with other couples occasionally, and over the years we have made some very deep friendships.

This was a challenge at first because it seemed if I liked the wife, Dan did not hit it off with the husband, or vice versa. Our couple friends are now well established, and we enjoy fellowship with these few couples. Life is busy if you are to meet the daily demands of marriage and family; a balance must be in place when it comes to friendships. We found it best suited us as well as our friends to socialize two to three times per year. Our greatest social network became involvement with our church. When we were raising children, our time was spent mostly around the activities of the youth groups our children attended. We faithfully attended an adult small group for years during our child-rearing years, which connected us with other believers. The small group had a range of adult believers who were older and younger, and we were able to spur one another on learning from each other.

Our greatest gift to one another is our time, meeting each other's needs as well as blessing one another. Look for ways to make the other's day better; this can only be done if you truly know your spouse. The following is a helpful, practical list of ways to get to know your spouse better (study your spouse) and connect with them in body, soul, mind, and spirit. Knowing your spouse is one way to build intimacy. If you are not married, some of this list may not apply yet because it is reserved for marriage.

What is your spouse's favorite[21]:
- Color
- Decorating style (such as traditional, contemporary, country, etc.)
- Car
- Activity
- House type
- Subject when they were in school
- City to visit
- Vacation destination
- Season of the year
- Least favorite season of the year
- Holiday
- Least favorite holiday
- Dessert
- Appetizer
- Entrée
- Meat
- Best friend
- Favorite relative
- Subject they like to discuss the most
- Favorite vacation they were ever on
- Favorite home-cooked meal
- Clothing store
- Favorite outfit
- Day of the week
- Most relaxing thing to do
- Movie
- Actor
- Book
- Music

- Sport
- Restaurant
- Book of the Bible
- Character of the Bible
- Verse of the Bible
- Sports team
- Sports hero
- Hobby
- Weather temperature
- Perfume/cologne
- Hair products
- Cleaning products
- Car products
- Vendors used for different services (such as dry cleaning, lawn care, servicing car etc.)

Do you know the following about your spouse?

- What stresses them the most
- Least favorite chore
- Pet peeve
- Shirt or blouse size
- Skirt or pants size
- Dress or suit size
- Shoe size
- One thing your spouse has dreamed of doing
- Type of vacation (relaxing, adventure, sightseeing, etc.)
- Greatest fear
- Greatest joy
- Kind of gift they like to receive
- Greatest dream to fulfill as couple
- If they could get paid for doing anything, what would be their dream job?

- Who would they love to meet if it were possible?
- If they could change anything they had ever done what would it be?
- Their greatest joy in life right now is?
- If they had a million dollars, what would they do with it?
- Where would they like to see your lives five years from now?
- What call has the Lord placed on their life?
- Their spiritual gifts are?
- Their greatest strengths
- Their greatest weakness
- How do they like to socialize?
- How does your spouse like you to flirt with them?
- How often do they like to make love?
- What is their favorite way of making love?
- What is their favorite place on their body to be touched?
- What ignites their passion?

Touch is very powerful. Learning how to touch without sex builds intimacy.

- Slow down! Life is already too fast paced
- Sit close to one another
- Hold hands
- Brush against each other lightly when passing by each other
- Hold hands when praying
- Massage head, neck, back, feet
- Snuggle when watching TV
- Sports that require touching each other
- Dance together
- Sleep naked in each other's arms
- Kissing the back of the neck
- Washing each other's hair or bodies
- Combing hair
- Undressing each other

Knowledge of the physical act of sexual intercourse is essential for a satisfying sexual relationship. Couples will assume this comes naturally; that is a fallacy. Making love is an art to be learned, and learning this art is a lifetime commitment. As we grow older our bodies change, and we must be willing to continue to learn and change as our bodies do. Other issues can also arise that affect the sexual relationship. Some of these issues do not show up immediately. The following list is a few areas of concern that could affect your sexual relationship. If these areas have not been dealt with, or proper healing has not taken place, seek professional counsel.

- Sexual impurity prior to marriage
- Rape, molestation, incest
- Pornography
- Parents who told children sex was dirty or wrong in efforts to encourage purity until marriage
- Parents who had unhealthy sex lives and children were aware of this
- Being physically abused

> "And the man and his wife were both naked and were not ashamed." Evidenced by these passages, you can clearly see that from the very beginning God intended man and woman to enjoy one another physically without shame in their nakedness. As their Creator, He intentionally designed their bodies to do so (Wheat & Wheat, 2001). Even more precious, Adam and Eve were to do this openly before Him. Powlison (1995) articulates, "God made sex. Adam and Eve went unclothed and celebrated a unity that was frankly physical…When the husband and wife join in intercourse, the One who sees in the dark sees exactly what they are doing and says, 'It is very good" (p. 1). You may be tempted to find this idea perverted or at minimum, inappropriate, especially since Christians often relate sex to words such as "dirty", "shameful", and "guilty" (McDonald & McDonald, 1996). However, if you are a Christian, you must seek to develop a biblical alternative to an otherwise lethal worldview of the physical union of husband and wife lest the joys and pleasures of this sacred gift be lost in the abyss of self-condemnation and sin.[22]

The following books are recommended reading in regard to the sexual relationship. These books deal specifically with the act of sex. We strongly encourage all couples to read these books. They are written by Christian authors and are very educational. For couples who are engaged, we recommend the male read these books only three weeks prior to marriage.

- *The Act of Marriage,* by Tim and Beverly LaHaye
- *Intended for Pleasure,* by Dr. Ed and Gayle Wheat
- *A Celebration of Sex After Fifty,* by Rosenau and Childerston

> Drink water from your own cistern, And running water from your own well. Should your fountains be dispersed abroad, Streams of water in the streets? Let them be only your own, And not for strangers with you. Let your fountain be blessed, And rejoice with the wife of your youth. As a loving deer and a graceful doe, Let her breasts satisfy you at all times; And always be enraptured with her love. For why should you, my son, be enraptured by an immoral woman, And be embraced in the arms of a seductress? For the ways of man are before the eyes of the LORD, And He ponders all his paths. His own iniquities entrap the wicked man, And he is caught in the cords of his sin. He shall die for lack of instruction, And in the greatness of his folly he shall go astray.
>
> Proverbs 5:15-21 (NKJV)

Foundational Stone Eight

As a husband I will put the following safeguards around myself and our sexual relationship to keep it pure:

_____

_____

_____

_____

_____

_____

_____

_____

_____

Foundational Stone Nine

As a wife I will put the following safeguards around myself and our sexual relationship to keep it pure:

_____

_____

_____

_____

_____

_____

_____

_____

> But my lover wouldn't take no for an answer, and the longer he knocked, the more excited I became. I got up to open the door to my lover, sweetly ready to receive him,
> Desiring and expectant as I turned the door handle.
>
> Song of Solomon 5:4-6a, (MSG)

Foundational Stone Ten

We will maintain intimacy in our marriage in the following ways:

_____

_____

_____

_____

_____

_____

_____

_____

_____

Place me like a seal over your heart, like a seal on your arm. For love is as strong as death, its jealousy as enduring as the grave. Love flashes like fire, the brightest kind of flame. Many waters cannot quench love, nor can rivers drown it. If a man tried to buy love with all his wealth, his offer would be utterly scorned.

Song of Solomon 8:6-7 (NLT)

The Torch of Tradition

> Wisdom is supreme; therefore get wisdom. Though it cost all you have, get understanding. He who gets wisdom loves his own soul; he who cherishes understanding prospers.
>
> Proverbs 4:7, 19:8 (NKJV)

The torch of tradition can either burn you or light your way depending on what that tradition was founded upon. A tradition can be anything from how basic tasks are done to the way we celebrate special days, or even the way we believe. Some of these traditions even dictate how we solve issues in life or react to a crisis. Normally traditions are passed down from one generation to the next.

Leaving and cleaving entitles us to form our own family unit. Some traditions are great assets to your marriage. Other traditions could be a possible determent, leading to constant conflict within your marriage. It is worth your while to study your family traditions and determine which ones are worth implementing into your marriage and which ones need to be thrown out with the trash. As couples, you may even want to establish some new traditions in your family unit. While we are to honor our father and mother, that does not mean we should allow them to pressure us into to doing things the way they do them.

First let's start with the basics. Determining how household tasks will be accomplished and who is responsible for these tasks is critical. Left undecided, this can be a huge area of conflict. The following is a list of basic household tasks or responsibilities. As you read through this list, think about how your parents took care of these tasks. Then as a couple determine who will be responsible for making sure these tasks are done. Will they be shared, rotated, or will one person take charge of a particular task? Responsibilities may need to change hands with different seasons of life. Seasons of life will come, and when they do, you must be willing to re-evaluate how things are done in your household (re-read chapter on the role of the wife).

Basic household tasks and responsibilities:
- Providing the income
- Paying the bills
- Finance and investments
- Stay with children or work outside of home
- Child care
- Meeting the needs of children: bathing, feeding, and changing diapers
- Dropping off/picking up children for activities or school events, doctor appointments, etc.
- Child discipline
- Spiritual education of children
- Helping with homework
- Cleaning house
- Making beds
- Home decorating
- Laundry
- Grocery shopping
- Meal preparation
- Trash
- Car maintenance
- Setting temperature of house
- House maintenance
- Lawn care/yard maintenance
- Snow removal
- Church attendance and activities
- Plan vacations
- Date nights

We Promise

- Discussing issues pertaining to family and relationship
- Personal education; whose education takes priority
- How days off and weekends are spent

How will your family celebrate the following days?
Special days and holidays:

- Birthdays
- Extended family birthdays
- New Year's
- Super Bowl
- Valentine's Day
- Easter
- Kentucky Derby
- Mother's Day
- Father's Day
- Memorial Day
- Fourth of July
- Labor Day
- Thanksgiving Day
- Christmas
- Any other day you regard as special

As you move forward to establish the family responsibilities and traditions you would like to form, or implement if you are already married, answering the following questions may help you.

When it comes to marriage, marital responsibilities and traditions, how have your individual families influenced you?

_____

_____

What are your expectations when it comes to finances and the use of credit cards, how has your family influenced you? How has the use of credit cards affected your marriage (if married)?

_____

_____

_____

What importance will or does mealtime have on you as a family?

_____

_____

_____

How did your family celebrate holidays? What traditions did they have? In your family, what traditions would you like to keep, and what would you like to add?

_____

_____

_____

When it comes to your extended family, how would you like to weave them into the traditions you are establishing for your own home?

_____

_____

Dan and I went into marriage pretty blindsided. We did not discuss any of the issues that are presented in this manual. Our pre-marriage counseling consisted of one meeting with our pastor prior to marriage. The only thing I remember discussing about our future was the type of house we would buy one day. As it turned out we did not buy or build the Swiss chalet we dreamed about.

Dan came from a traditional churched home. They lived in a standard ranch in the suburbs. His family attended church weekly and his mom was a stay-at-home mother. Their traditions were solid, and there was a great emphasis on food not only at family gatherings but also at mealtimes. I was a very small-town girl. My father was a carpenter, and my mother worked full-time in a factory. During most of my childhood years, she worked second shift, and I only saw her on the weekends. My dad did all the grocery shopping and cooking of meals. My parents did not attend church, and as a little girl, I walked alone to the local Baptist church each Sunday. I also took part in Pioneer Girls and youth events.

I can remember the first time I made supper for my husband. After supper was finished, he wanted to know where the dessert was. In his house growing up, they had dessert with every evening meal. In my house we never had dessert, and if we did, it was ice cream on a rare occasion or a cake during a birthday celebration. My father was a union carpenter, and we were not allowed to eat at fast food places because he said they were built by scab labor. Until I was sixteen and had my own job, I had not eaten at McDonald's, Wendy's, or Pizza Hut (I think you get the picture). The first year of college for me was a real awakening to foods, and it did not take long for me to realize I was packing on some pounds; fortunately, I recognized the issue and got it under control. The weight issue meant a clothes issue, so being a poor college student, I had to respect the fact that buying clothes was not in the budget. After marrying Dan, once again, I was plagued with more food discoveries. All I can say is, it's a good thing I'm an active person.

When Dan entered into marriage with the expectation of dessert with each evening meal, I was totally shocked and could not understand why anyone needed dessert with every supper, and this was not his only expectation. Christmas our first year of marriage also gave me a big revelation. As Christmas drew nearer, Dan asked me when I was planning on making Christmas cookies. Now you must understand, my mother never cooked, and no one taught me how to cook or bake. I was flying by the seat of my pants when it came to the cooking department. Dan loaded me in the car that week, informing me we were going to Meijer's and buying everything needed to make Christmas cookies. This of course not only included the ingredients for the cookies but the cookie cutters and baking sheets. Fortunately for me my grandmother was a great cook. I called Grandma Rosie and was able to obtain all her prize cookie recipes. Grandma Rosie became a source for recipes, as well as Betty Crocker. When you hear the saying "the way to a man's heart is through his stomach," there is truth to that. I was determined to make my man happy, and one of those ways was through food. There is another saying my husband likes better, and it is, "Come naked. Bring food."

Very quickly I became aware of how little I knew about my husband's traditions. These traditions not only encompassed *food*, which I already discussed, but also chores, responsibilities, and his definition of what the roles of husband and wife were. I felt as though I were along for the ride. I realized my family did little to instill wholesome family living, and I had a lot to learn. I also knew I did not necessarily care for all of *his* traditions; I felt it put great demands on me that I did not know if I could live up to.

One of my husband's traditions that he expected me to follow through on was sending everyone in his family, including cousins, aunts, and uncles, a birthday card. Dan was also big on sending out hundreds of Christmas cards. The problem was, at first he thought I should take care of all the card issues. After several years of failing in this area and Dan checking up on me, I came to the conclusion that if he wanted to send all these cards out, it needed to be his job, not mine! Why I waited so many years to express that I hated the card job, I do not know.

The fact is, I have a very serving, pleasing temperament. Dan had a strong military background. When we were first married, he was fulfilling a commitment to the Army National Guard, which eventually placed him as the commander of the 1073rd Army National Guard Unit. There were times throughout our marriage where I needed to remind him I was not one of his soldiers, that I was indeed his wife and should not be ordered around. My husband thinks I have overcome the weak area in my life of letting people take advantage of me and I have no problem voicing my concerns now. He says I am now like the woman in *Dances With Wolves*, Stands with a Fist. I think I like that! Personally, I think he likes it too. Dan knows he took advantage of me in those early years, but he did not like others taking advantage of me either.

I must admit, Dan was not the only one who came with expectations into the marriage. I also had some very unrealistic expectations of Dan, and still to this day I must remind myself that is exactly what they are, unrealistic. My father and brother could fix anything. They would be what you consider as millwrights, the jacks of all trades. When it came to cars, plumbing, electrical, carpentry, cement, small engines, you name it, they could fix it. Dan was taught none of these talents growing up and didn't care to learn them after he became a man. Now I must say he gave gallant efforts because I pushed him, but in the end it always cost us more money to fix the blunders, if they were fixable at all. My husband has many qualities that are fabulous; however, being a jack of all trades is not one of them. Being a carpenter's daughter, I tried my hand at many home improvement projects as well, to my husband's dismay, after he had begged me to hire those jobs done.

One prime example is the oak wood floor in the foyer of our house. I was quoted over fifteen hundred dollars to have the floor refinished. I thought that was ridiculous. I could surely rent the equipment, sand, and finish it myself. When Dan came home from work and saw the pile of sawdust lying on the ground outside, he knew we were in big trouble. He was scared to walk in the house, and at that point I didn't want him to see the disaster I had created either. I am definitely a tightwad, and hiring people to get things done just goes against my nature (Lord, help me!). I am so thankful we grew, matured, and were able to truly make our house a home, dying to ourselves and learning to put the other first. We are now empty nesters who completely enjoy each other's company as best friends as well as lovers.

When it comes to establishing traditions in your family, uniqueness is a fun ingredient. Together you can develop memories that will last for a lifetime. To give you an example, Dan and I coded our Christmas presents to the children. When the girls were young and the presents were under the tree, they were able to guess what they got for Christmas by the shape and size of the boxes. This drove me crazy because I wanted them to be surprised. So I began to code the presents. Each year I used a different code. Some of the codes I used were favorite colors, sports, themes, social security numbers, and Bible verses. The person who was able to break the code by Christmas Day would get a sum of money. The girls would never tell if they figured out the code prior to Christmas because that person wanted the money, so mum was the word. One tradition the girls did enjoy was that on Christmas morning, we would have homemade pecan sticky buns. To this day if the girls come for Christmas, they expect the pecan sticky buns to be there waiting for them.

To conclude this chapter, coming together and discovering each other's expectations in regard to responsibilities and traditions is a vital stone for happiness. Happiness, as we understand it, is when a person feels good about something. But true happiness, in biblical understanding, is more of an action, as we'll see in the same Hebrew and Greek word *blessed*. *Blessed*[23] means to be straight, especially to be level, right happy. To go forward, be honest and proper. To guide, lead, relieve. Happy, fortunate, to be envied. Biblical happiness depends more on our doing then on our feelings. The way we think about others and ourselves will make us happy or sad. Be blessed by thinking straight, level, right, and happy.[24] The daily routines of chores as well as special occasions have to be accomplished, so we might as well find a way to see these areas through with joy in our hearts. *Action behind right motives will produce positive results.* We must be sure in the everyday things of life that we do not allow the little foxes to steal our grapes. We are reminded of this in Song of Solomon 2:15 (NKJV), "Catch us the foxes, the little foxes that spoil the vines, for our vines have tender grapes."

Foundational Stone Eleven

> Through wisdom a house is built, And by understanding it is established.
> Proverbs 24:3 (NKJV)

We will establish the following routines, chores, and traditions in our home:

_____

_____

_____

_____

_____

_____

_____

_____

_____

Clashing Cymbals

> If I speak in the tongues of men and of angels, but have not love, I am only a resounding gong or a clanging cymbal.
>
> 1 Corinthians 13:1 (NIV)

Endeavoring to resolve issues can be like the clashing of two cymbals together that are out of sync with the music. When cymbals are brought together at the appropriate time during a concert, they add a beautiful climax to the symphony being played; however, clash them at the wrong moment, and it can destroy the symphony. We have heard it said "it's all in the timing," and this is true when it comes to resolving conflict.

Many facets come into play when resolving conflict. Mastering two of the greatest principles of our faith will enable us not only to resolve conflict but also allow us to live in harmony. Repentance and forgiveness are paramount in our life if we want to be able to resolve conflict and establish good communication skills. Without repentance and forgiveness, there will be no lasting resolution to issues couples may face. Entering into marriage with an unrepentant heart full of unforgiveness can sabotage your relationship, even if those issues had nothing to do with your spouse. This not only affects you individually, it will affect your relationships with others who may have had nothing to do with the incidents that took place.

Repentance is taking responsibility for wrongful actions in thought, word, or deed, and confessing of that wrongdoing and changing your behavior as to not repeat that sin again. In a day where sin is not called sin but a mistake, how is it possible to know what true repentance is? A mistake is: I subtracted incorrectly in my checkbook; I poured bleach in the washer instead of the laundry detergent; I wrote my doctor's appointment down on my calendar on the wrong day; I forgot to pick up my kids from school; I backed into the garbage can; I sent the electric bill in and left the check to pay for it in the checkbook; and on we could go. But the Bible has a definition for sin; many scriptures in the Bible leave no room to say it is a gray area. Sin is sin, and that is the bottom line.

> Sin: to do wrong deliberately
>
> Iniquity: wickedness; wrongful act; unjust
>
> Transgression: to break; to go beyond the limits; to violate[25]

Everyone would agree that if you were to break one of the Ten Commandments, that would be sin. But the Ten Commandments are not the only place in Scripture where sin is defined. Throughout all of the Old and New Testament, guidelines for righteous living (living right without sin) can be found. In the Fifty-first Psalm, David takes responsibility for his action of sin. Acknowledgment of the sin is the first step; taking responsibility for sin must follow. Confession of sin and a change in behavior that allowed the sin to take place sets in motion the right attitude for permanent change to take place, allowing for righteous living. God always calls us to repentance. Conviction of sin may come through various avenues such as our conscience, getting caught, or a fellow believer bringing the issue to our attention. One thing for sure is, our sin is always disclosed, and we will always be given the opportunity to repent, confess, and make amends for our behavior or actions. We cannot hide our sin. Read what the Word of God has to say about hidden sin.

> Therefore do not fear them. For there is nothing covered that will not be revealed, and hidden that will not be known.
>
> Matthew 10:26 (NKJV)

> For there is nothing hidden which will not be revealed, nor has anything been kept secret but that it should come to light.
>
> Mark 4:22 (NKJV)

> For nothing is secret that will not be revealed, nor anything hidden that will not be known and come to light.
>
> Luke 8:17 (NKJV)

> For there is nothing covered that will not be revealed, nor hidden that will not be known.
>
> Luke 12:2 (NKJV)

And thus the secrets of his heart are revealed; and so, falling down on his face, he will worship God and report that God is truly among you.

1 Corinthians 14:25 (NKJV)

Therefore thus says the Lord GOD: Because you have made your iniquity to be remembered, in that your transgressions are uncovered, so that in all your doings your sins appear; because you have come to remembrance, you shall be taken in hand.

Ezekiel 21:24 (NKJV)

Many times we wonder why our prayers are not answered. The Bible gives us insight with the following passages:

When you spread out your hands in prayer, I will hide my eyes from you; even if you offer many prayers, I will not listen. Your hands are full of blood; *wash and make yourselves clean. Take your evil deeds out of my sight! Stop doing wrong,* learn to do right! Seek justice, encourage the oppressed. Defend the cause of the fatherless, plead the case of the widow. "Come now, let us reason together," says the LORD. "Though your sins are like scarlet, they shall be as white as snow; though they are red as crimson, they shall be like wool. If you are *willing and obedient*, you will eat the best from the land; but if you resist and rebel, you will be devoured by the sword." For the mouth of the LORD has spoken.

Isaiah 1:15-20 (NIV)

But your *iniquities have separated you from your God; your sins have hidden his face from you, so that he will not hear.*

Isaiah 59:2 (NIV)

When you ask, you do not receive, because you ask with wrong motives, that you may spend what you get on your pleasures.

James 4:3 (NIV)

Husbands, in the same way be considerate as you live with your wives, and treat them with respect as the weaker partner and as heirs with you of the gracious gift of life, so that nothing will hinder your prayers.

1 Peter 3:7 (NIV)

> And receive from him anything we ask, *because we obey his commands and do what pleases him.*
>
> 1 John 3:22 (NIV)

What hinders our prayers from being heard?

_____

Studying Psalm 51 along with other scriptures will help us to recognize what true repentance is. Did David take responsibility for his sin? What did he call the sin he committed? What did David declare the Lord desires? What did David ask God to change in Him? What did David say he will do after he is restored? Did David place blame on anyone else?

_____

_____

_____

_____

_____

Study the following scriptures:

> Therefore, O house of Israel, I will judge you, each one according to his ways, declares the Sovereign Lord. *Repent! Turn away from all your offenses; then sin will not be your downfall. Rid yourselves of all the offenses you have committed, and get a new heart and a new spirit.* Why will you die, O house of Israel? For I take no pleasure in the death of anyone, declares the Sovereign Lord. *Repent and live!*
>
> Ezekiel 18:30-32 NIV

Now, brothers, I know that you acted in ignorance, as did your leaders. But this is how God fulfilled what he had foretold through all the prophets, saying that his Christ would suffer. *Repent, then, and turn to God, so that your sins may be wiped out, that times of refreshing may come from the Lord,* and that he may send the Christ, who has been appointed for you—even Jesus.

Acts 3:17-20 (NIV)

Now the tax collectors and "sinners" were all gathering around to hear him. But the Pharisees and the teachers of the law muttered, "This man welcomes sinners and eats with them." Then Jesus told them this parable: "Suppose one of you has a hundred sheep and loses one of them. Does he not leave the ninety-nine in the open country and go after the lost sheep until he finds it? And when he finds it, he joyfully puts it on his shoulders and goes home. Then he calls his friends and neighbors together and says, 'Rejoice with me; I have found my lost sheep.' I tell you that in the same way *there will be more rejoicing in heaven over one sinner who repents than over ninety-nine righteous persons who do not need to repent.*"

Luke 15:1-7 (NIV)

But because of your stubbornness and your *unrepentant* heart, *you are storing up wrath against yourself* for the day of God's wrath, when his righteous judgment will be revealed. God will give to each person according to what he has done. To those who by persistence in doing good seek glory, honor and immortality, he will give eternal life. But for those who are self-seeking and who reject the truth and follow evil, there will be wrath and anger. *There will be trouble and distress for every human being who does evil:* first for the Jew, then for the Gentile.

Romans 2:5-9 (NIV)

And saying, "*Repent,* for the kingdom of heaven is at hand!"

Matthew 3:2 (NKJV)

From that time Jesus began to preach and to say, "*Repent,* for the kingdom of heaven is at hand."

Matthew 4:17 (NKJV)

Remember therefore from where you have fallen; *repent* and do the first works, or else I will come to you quickly and remove your lampstand from its place; unless you *repent*.

Revelation 2:5 (NKJV)

Repent, or else I will come to you quickly and will fight against them with the sword of My mouth.

Revelation 2:16 (NKJV)

And I gave her time to *repent* of her sexual immorality, and she did not *repent*.

Revelation 2:21 (NKJV)

Indeed I will cast her into a sickbed, and those who commit adultery with her into great tribulation, unless they *repent* of their deeds.

Revelation 2:22 (NKJV)

Remember therefore how you have received and heard; hold fast and *repent*. Therefore if you will not watch, I will come upon you as a thief, and you will not know what hour I will come upon you.

Revelation 3:3 (NKJV)

As many as I love, I rebuke and chasten. Therefore be zealous and *repent*.

Revelation 3:19 (NKJV)

After studying these verses, do you understand the importance God places on repentance? How will an unrepentant heart affect your life and your marital relationship? When we do repent what does God say will occur? What will occur if we do not repent?

_____

_____

_____

_____

We Promise

According to Psalm 119:59, how can we recognize we are sinning?

_____

Study the following scriptures to discover how others can influence our behavior and the decisions we make.

> Do not be yoked together with unbelievers. For what do righteousness and wickedness have in common? Or what fellowship can light have with darkness? What harmony is there between Christ and Belial ? What does a believer have in common with an unbeliever? What agreement is there between the temple of God and idols? For we are the temple of the living God. As God has said: "I will live with them and walk among them, and I will be their God, and they will be my people." *Therefore, "come out from them and be separate, says the Lord. Touch no unclean thing, and I will receive you."* And "I will be a Father to you, and you will be my sons and daughters, says the Lord Almighty."
>
> 2 Corinthians 6:14-18 (NIV)

What has the Lord asked us to do according to 2 Corinthians 6:14-18?

_____

_____

_____

> He keeps company with evildoers; he associates with wicked men.
>
> Job 34:8 (NIV)

> All have turned aside, they have together become corrupt; there is no one who does good, not even one. Will evildoers never learn-- those who devour my people as men eat bread and who do not call on the LORD? There they are, overwhelmed with dread, *for God is present in the company of the righteous.*
>
> Psalm 14:3-5 (NIV)

> Do not be misled: "Bad company corrupts good character."
>
> 1 Corinthians 15:33 (NIV)

Do you think the company you keep affects you? How does it affect you personally?

_____

_____

Read Ephesians 4:22-32, Ephesians 5:1-19, and Colossians 3:1-17 and answer the following questions:

What are the characteristics of ungodly living? Is this sin?

_____

_____

_____

_____

What are the attributes of Godly living? Is this righteous living?

_____

_____

_____

_____

Are there areas in your life that you can identify from the Scriptures you read that you need to repent from? What are these areas? What changes must you make in your life to make sure you do not fall back into sin? Do you want to repent and be in right standing with God?

_____

_____

_____

_____

"Godly sorrow brings repentance that leads to salvation and leaves no regret, but worldly sorrow brings death" (2 Corinthians 7:10, NIV). As an individual or couple, coming clean or repenting of any un-confessed sin will help set the stage for lasting resolution to conflicts and create harmony in living.

Forgiveness is the next attribute we must examine thoroughly in our individual lives as well as in our couple lives to be able to establish healthy conflict resolution, which has lasting effects. "To forgive is to set the prisoner free, then discover the prisoner was you" (Author unknown). A careful study of Matthew 18 will bring a greater awareness of the importance our Lord places on forgiveness. Please bear in mind this parable is about unforgiveness. The scriptures written prior to and after the parable deal directly with unforgiveness and its implications.

> Then Peter came up and said to him, "Lord, how often will my brother sin against me, and I forgive him? As many as seven times?" Jesus said to him, "I do not say to you seven times, but seventy times seven. "Therefore the kingdom of heaven may be compared to a king who wished to settle accounts with his servants. When he began to settle, one was brought to him who owed him ten thousand talents. And since he could not pay, his master ordered him to be sold, with his wife and children and all that he had, and payment to be made. So the servant fell on his knees, imploring him, 'Have patience with me, and I will pay you everything.' And out of pity for him, the master of that servant released him and forgave him the debt. But when that same servant went out, he found one of his fellow servants who owed him a hundred denarii, and seizing him, he began to choke him, saying, 'Pay

what you owe.' So his fellow servant fell down and pleaded with him, 'Have patience with me, and I will pay you.' He refused and went and put him in prison until he should pay the debt. When his fellow servants saw what had taken place, they were greatly distressed, and they went and reported to their master all that had taken place. Then his master summoned him and said to him, 'You wicked servant! I forgave you all that debt because you pleaded with me. And should not you have had mercy on your fellow servant, as I had mercy on you?' And in anger his master delivered him to the jailers, until he should pay all his debt. So also my heavenly Father will do to every one of you, if you do not forgive your brother from your heart."

Matthew 18:21-35 (ESV)

One day I was reading the Word and came across verse 21. I stopped and prayed and asked the Lord. Who would sin the same sin against someone seventy times seven. The Lord began to impress upon me a great truth. It was not necessarily that they sinned against you seventy times seven; it was that after you forgave them you took it back, again and again and again. You see, when we make the effort to forgive someone, it's a choice. Then the enemy comes back with a baiting thought, reminding you of that sin or offense. At that moment you have a choice. You can either send the thought packing, telling the devil you forgave that person and it is settled, or you can dwell on the thought, build a nest in your brain, let that bird (thought) sit on its eggs, and hatch them! As these eggs begin to hatch, there are other offenses this person may have committed. You begin to make a list of them, and it gets longer! You have now taken back your forgiveness toward this person. I encourage you to ponder the following breakdown of these verses in Mathew 18. Remember, this parable is about forgiveness.

- Verse 25: the servant was unable to pay, so he *and his entire family* and all that he had was to be sold to pay this debt.
- Verse 27: the master took pity and released him from the debt (Jesus paid a debt for us that we could never pay).
- Verses 28-30: the servant is unwilling to release another from a debt that was owed.
- Verses 32-34: the master is very upset that he had canceled the debt of the servant, but the servant was not willing to cancel the debt of another. The servant was turned over to the jailers to be tortured (the NIV and NKJV translations use the word *tortured* and *torturers*) until he paid back what he owed (he owed forgiveness to another).
- Verse 35: unless we are willing to forgive our brother, we will be treated the same as this wicked servant was: turned over to the jailers to be tortured.

We Promise

Because God has forgiven us through the death and resurrection of Jesus paying the once-and-for-all sacrifice (read Hebrews 5:7-10), we are called to forgive others. Studying the following scriptures will support this statement:

> Forgive us our debts, as we also have forgiven our debtors. And lead us not into temptation, but deliver us from the evil one.' For if you forgive men when they sin against you, your heavenly Father will also forgive you. But if you do not forgive men their sins, your Father will not forgive your sins.
>
> Matthew 6:12-15 (NIV)

> This is how my heavenly Father will treat each of you unless you forgive your brother from your heart.
>
> Matthew 18:35 (NIV)

> "Therefore I say to you, whatever things you ask when you pray, believe that you receive them, and you will have them. "And whenever you stand praying, if you have anything against anyone, forgive him, that your Father in heaven may also forgive you your trespasses. "But if you do not forgive, neither will your Father in heaven forgive your trespasses."
>
> Mark 11:24-26 (NKJV)

> Forgive us our sins, for we also forgive everyone who sins against us. And lead us not into temptation.
>
> Luke 11:4 (NIV)

As you can see, it is very clear that if we want forgiveness, we must be willing to forgive. Answer the following questions now that you have reflected upon what forgiveness is.

Do you think unforgiveness is evil? Express your thoughts on this. Do you think unforgiveness is a sin? Is sin evil? What will happen according to the Bible if you do not forgive? What physical, emotional, or spiritual torment could you suffer if you do not forgive? What have you experienced in the past?

_____

_____

According to 1 John 1:8, we have deceived ourselves if we claim to be without sin. Is it possible that you have lived with unforgiveness in your heart toward someone for so long that you have become blinded to its presence? Why not pause right now and ask the Holy Spirit to bring to your mind anyone whom you have not forgiven. Are you ready to take that step now and truly forgive?[26]

_____

_____

In my personal walk with the Lord, when He has brought something to my attention that is sin, I need to repent, forgive, change, or whatever else is required to overcome that sin. Something I have noticed is that I do not always want to do this. I must choose to act on obedience and do it anyway. The Lord always acknowledges my act of obedience and eventually catches my emotions or feelings up to the act of obedience, and it becomes well with my soul. This may take a few days or even months of faithfully walking in the act of repentance and forgiveness. There have been times in my life where I have kept awareness about me that a particular issue is sin, and I must hate it. I have had to talk myself into hating it, reminding myself of all the consequences of that sin. I have to replace those strong thoughts or urges of *stinkin' thinkin'*. When this is a forgiveness issue, God simply asks us to forgive; He does not ask us to forget. Forgetting is impossible; it is part of our history. Notice I said *history*; it happened, it's in the past, but it doesn't have the right to dictate our future unless we let it. We must guard our minds so as to not let old thoughts come back in; we must truly put on the helmet of salvation.

Look up the following scriptures and identify how we are to respond to others who have offended us.

Proverbs 10:12

_____

Proverbs 17:9

_____

We Promise

Proverbs 19:11

_____

Luke 6:27-31

_____

Luke 17:3-4

_____

Romans 12:17-21

_____

1 Corinthians 13:4-7

_____

Colossians 3:13

_____

Romans 12:19

_____

1 Peter 4:8

_____

Jude 1:22-23 (NLT)

_____

Once we have taken the steps to forgive, we must guard our minds, putting in place boundaries for our thinking process. Scripture has a plan for us. Study the following verses. Applying these verses will enable us in winning the battle that can rage in our minds as it pertains to others and offenses.

> *Let this mind be in you which was also in Christ Jesus*, who, being in the form of God, did not consider it robbery to be equal with God, but made Himself of no reputation, taking the form of a bondservant, *and* coming in the likeness of men. And being found in appearance as a man, He humbled Himself and became obedient to *the point of* death, even the death of the cross.
>
> Philippians 2:5-8 (NKJV)

> Be anxious for nothing, but in everything by prayer and supplication, with thanksgiving, let your requests be made known to God; and the peace of God, which surpasses all understanding, will guard your hearts and minds through Christ Jesus. Finally, brethren, whatever things are true, whatever things *are* noble, whatever things *are* just, whatever things *are* pure, whatever things *are* lovely, whatever things *are* of good report, if *there is* any virtue and if *there is* anything praiseworthy—*meditate on these things*. The things which you learned and received and heard and saw in me, these do, and the God of peace will be with you.
>
> Philippians 4:6-8 (NKJV)

> Therefore, since Christ suffered for us in the flesh, *arm yourselves also with the same mind*, for he who has suffered in the flesh has ceased from sin, that he no longer should live the rest of *his* time in the flesh for the lusts of men, but for the will of God.
>
> 1 Peter 4:1-2 (NKJV)

> For to be carnally minded *is* death, but to be spiritually minded is life and peace. Because the carnal mind *is* enmity against God; for it is not subject to the law of God, nor indeed can be.
>
> Romans 8:6-7 (NKJV)

Before we move into conflict resolution, there is another concept I would like to make you aware of. We all have people in our lives, that no matter what we do, we must be cautious not to set them off. We feel as though we are walking on egg shells; they may be members of our family, coworkers, even those with whom we serve in a ministry, but what we fail to recognize is our shoestrings are untied, and we are stepping on them.

We Promise

The Bible has charged us to "make every effort to live in peace with all men and to be holy; without holiness no one will see the Lord" (Hebrews 12:14, NIV). The New King James Version says, "Pursue peace with all people, and holiness, without which no one will see the Lord." Pursue means to press toward; peace means one, peace, quietness, rest, and set at one again. We are given this charge, but how on earth can we accomplish this? Most of us are unprepared; we have left our shoe strings untied, and it is time for us to tie up the loose ends in our lives so we can be effective in ministering to the hurting lives of others.

I had a personal experience once that brought about this concept. I contract with a large company in which I teach CPR/AED/First Aid. I have worked for this company for many years. Unfortunately, almost every year they seem to change my contact person with whom arrangements are made for trainings. One year my contact person was Carol. Carol was making my life miserable with her constant questioning of how these classes were taught, set up, and billed, etc. Now I had been working with this company rather smoothly for years. There were no issues, and everything came together very nicely. As I began to show up at trainings, I realized this woman was not well liked among other employees at this large institution. She rubbed others the wrong way and made things more difficult than need be. I began to get anxious whenever I saw her number on caller ID because I knew it would be another complaint or nervousness on her part that everything would be done right.

The solution: I began to pray for Carol and asked the Lord what I could do to bring some kind of joy into her life of complaints. One day I realized Carol had been sick; she dealt with very severe asthma and allergy issues. These issues dominated her life, making her miserable day in and day out. One day when Carol was experiencing severe symptoms, I asked if I could pray for her healing. She responded she would be grateful for that. This small gesture began to turn Carol's attitude toward me around. Our conversations were pleasant, and she was less panicked each time she called or e-mailed me. I began to encourage her for the good job she was doing following up on everything, instead of thinking she did not trust me. For the rest of my encounters with Carol, they were pleasant and not threatening.

After having this experience, my daughter was having a difficult time with her supervisor (no one liked this man). I shared with her my story about Carol and encouraged her to pray for this man, his job, and his well-being. She took my advice, and his attitude began to change. He took a liking to my daughter, and when semi-annual reviews came around, she got an above excellent that brought her a raise and opportunities at her place of employment. Although he is not her supervisor anymore, he continues to put in good words for my daughter and the career she is pursuing at her place of employment.

As believers, what we fail to realize is people are hurting. They react out of that hurt. We as believers need to find ways to bring the love of Christ Jesus into their lives. Acts of kindness can go a long way, even if we do not want to be kind to someone who is making us miserable. Let's look to the Word now for biblical examples of how to treat others.

> It is to a man's honor to avoid strife, but every fool is quick to quarrel.
>
> Proverbs 20:3 (NIV)

> The purposes of a man's heart are deep waters, but a man of understanding draws them out.
>
> Proverbs 20:5 (NIV)

The Lord wants all of us to be drawn out of deep waters.

> He reached down from on high and took hold of me; he drew me out of deep waters. He rescued me from my powerful enemy, from my foes, who were too strong for me.
>
> Psalm 18:16-17 (NIV)

Our words do have merit and life, or they can cause great harm.

> He who guards his mouth and his tongue keeps himself from calamity.
>
> Proverbs 21:23 (NIV)

> With the tongue we praise our Lord and Father, and with it we curse men, who have been made in God's likeness. Out of the same mouth come praise and cursing. My brothers, this should not be. Can both fresh water and salt water flow from the same spring? My brothers, can a fig tree bear olives, or a grapevine bear figs? Neither can a salt spring produce fresh water. But the wisdom that comes from heaven is first of all pure; then peace-loving, considerate, submissive, full of mercy and good fruit, impartial and sincere.
>
> James 3:9-12,17 (NIV)

> Starting a quarrel is like breaching a dam; so drop the matter before a dispute breaks out.
>
> Proverbs 17:14 (NIV)

We Promise

> He who loves a quarrel loves sin; he who builds a high gate invites destruction.
>
> Proverbs 17:19 (NIV)

> A cheerful heart is good medicine, but a crushed spirit dries up the bones.
>
> Proverbs 17:22 (NIV)

> A man of knowledge uses words with restraint, and a man of understanding is even-tempered.
>
> Proverbs 17:27 (NIV)

> He who answers before listening—that is his folly and his shame. A man's spirit sustains him in sickness, but a crushed spirit who can bear?
>
> Proverbs 18:13-14 (NIV)

> The tongue has the power of life and death, and those who love it will eat its fruit.
>
> Proverbs 18:21 (NIV)

> He who gets wisdom loves his own soul; he who cherishes understanding prospers.
>
> Proverbs 19:8 (NIV)

> A man's wisdom gives him patience; *it is to his glory to overlook an offense.*
>
> Proverbs 19:11 (NIV)

> He who is kind to the poor lends to the LORD, and he will reward him for what he has done.
>
> Proverbs 19:17 (NIV)

Conflict Resolution

Disclaimer: Domestic violence is a grave darkness. As many as one in four women are a victim of domestic violence.[27] These stats are the same for the churched as well as the un-churched. Submission principles as well as conflict resolution will not work in domestic violence. Safety is of the utmost importance. God never intended a woman to be covered with violence. Read Psalm 55 and Malachi 2:14-16. For more information on domestic violence visit: www.abigails.org and www.ndvh.org. If you are a victim of domestic violence, do not access these websites from your home computer. Two great resources for reading written by Dr. Paul Hegstrom: *Angry Men and the Women Who Love Them* and *Broken Children, Grown-Up Pain*. Dr. Paul Hegstrom is the founder of Life Skills International, www.lifeskillsintl.org.[28]

Now that we have obtained knowledge in the area of repentance, forgiveness, and acts of kindness to others, we are ready to learn how to apply conflict resolution. First we must ask ourselves why we would even have to apply conflict resolution when it comes to our marriage. In James 4:1-3 (NKJV) the answer to this question is revealed.

> Where do wars and fights come from among you? *Do they not come from your desires for pleasure that war in your members? You lust and do not have. You murder and covet and cannot obtain. You fight and war.* Yet you do not have because you do not ask. You ask and do not receive, because you ask amiss, *that you may spend it on your pleasures.*

Our human nature is very self-centered, which is why the Bible encourages us to die to self and put others first. As we grow and mature in the Lord and in years, we learn the great necessity of dying to self. Unfortunately, even the most spiritually mature person will succumb to the flesh and need to apply conflict resolution to their marriage. We all deal with anger from time to time. Some people have learned to control this emotion; others let anger control them. Anger is a secondary emotion. There is always an underlying cause. We must choose as individuals to control anger and not let it control us. Because anger is internally created, it can be internally managed. The anger often stems from an unmet expectation that was unrealistic in nature. Anger in and of itself is not sin. How we express anger determines whether or not we sin.

According to Ephesians 4:26-27 (NKJV) it says, "Be angry, and do not sin': do not let the sun go down on your wrath, nor give place to the devil." Couples must make a plan on how they are going to resolve issues in a mature manner that does not break down or destroy the other person. We must make ourselves adapt a calmer lifestyle. Many times a release of anger in outburst has nothing to do with why we are really angry. We take advantage of the opportunity to let off steam usually with the one we love, even if they had nothing to do with why we are really angry. We express anger toward this person because it is convenient, instead of dealing with our emotions and searching our hearts as to why we are upset or angry.

The first step in conflict resolution is to analyze ourselves. We all have physical signs in our bodies that take place when we start to become angry. Some of the physical characteristics a person may have are: sweaty hands or face, dry mouth, tension headache, nausea, heartburn, tight jaw, confusion, red face, uncontrolled chattering, and laughing inappropriately, to name a few. Do you recognize any of these in yourself? At the first sign of your physical indictor of anger, you must call for a time out. A time out is when both individuals agree to separate for a time of self-searching and analysis of your motives. This is a time to seek the Lord. Conflict resolution will only work if both individuals agree to apply it. If one person calls a time out and the other person is following them with an avalanche of words, this is not a time out. The following steps are to help to formulate a conflict resolution of your own as a couple. We suggest you write out your own resolution that you both agree to abide by in times of conflict or disagreement.

Resolution Steps:

- Take a time out! This is a learned behavior to delay your reactions. The minute you feel the escalation of emotions leading to anger or realize physical signs in your body, you need to take a time out. Examine what you are feeling. Are you experiencing hurt, rejection, helplessness, shame, or guilt?
- Identify your feelings. How upset are you, and where could these feelings lead?

Put your actions, attitudes, words, or decisions to a test:

1. Will this draw us closer or drive us apart?
2. Will it build up or tear down our relationship?
3. Will it bring about a positive response or a negative response?
4. Does it express my love and loyalty to my partner, or does it reveal my self-centered individualism?[29]

- Recognize the real cause of the anger. What triggered it? What were the issues that brought on these emotions you're dealing with right now? What is the reality or truth of the situation?
- Examine the anger. Is the anger justified, or did you incorrectly perceive the circumstance? Step back from the situation. Because of wounds of childhood, there are times that your sensitivities, fears, anxieties, and rejection may lead you to perceive or believe things that are not necessarily reality.
- Meditate through the situation. Do not take action until you have given thought to all that has occurred and you have control of your responses, reactions, and words.

- Resolve the conflict or issues after contemplating clearly and recognizing the reality of the conflict. Confront calmly, set boundaries and healthy limits, obtain wise counsel, express your feelings (using I statements, not you), negotiate resolution, compromise, or agree to deal with the issues at a later time. You can simply let go and forgive. You have absolutely no control over other people or circumstances.
- Forgive. Forgiveness releases you from the mental vice of the person who offended or treated you poorly. Forgiveness does not condone the behavior of others who offend. Trust must be earned and regained.[30]

During a time out, seek the Lord and wait on Him to reveal the issues of your heart. Do not drive or drink coffee, alcohol, or other beverages that increase the heart rate. Do not call your friends or parents. This is a time to examine the situation and your response to what has occurred. Time outs are normally thirty to sixty minutes in length. If you are unable to meet together after sixty minutes, agree to a time frame when you and your spouse will be able to discuss and resolve the matter in a calm, peaceful fashion, hearing what each other has to say. After one person has spoken and expressed themselves using I statements, the other person should repeat what they said, making sure the person speaking was perceived and understood correctly. The person listening repeats what they heard, saying, for example: "If I heard and perceived you correctly, you said…" This should help alleviate any misunderstandings or misconceptions.

Assertiveness is expressing your feelings forthrightly in a healthy loving way. This is the best method to direct your anger. Most people are very indirect when it comes to expressing themselves. Your parents' influence on you as you grew up may have led you to believe it was selfish to talk about yourself. In addition to this, you could have been disciplined unfairly when you tried to express your feelings. The outcome of such discipline has created a fear of being able to directly express yourself. You may even allow others to dominate the resolution of conflict or put words in your mouth. Learning new skills on how to resolve conflict will alleviate hidden anger and frustration. Assertiveness is biblical! Paul writes about the value of "speaking the truth in love" and "speaking truthfully to your neighbor" in Ephesians 4:15 and 29.

In John 4:17-18, Jesus said to the Samaritan woman, "You are right when you say you have no husband. The fact is, you have had five husbands, and the man you now have is not your husband" (NIV). Pretty direct, huh?[31]

- Ask for God's Intervention: Pray for God's leading through Scripture and His Holy Spirit. Ask Him to help you proclaim the truth in love.

- **S**tate the problem. Think over and acknowledge the facts of the problem and concerns.
- Express yourself. State your feelings.
- Request change and feedback. Specify one behavioral alteration. Then listen to the other person's concerns and opinions.
- Talk it out: paraphrase their ideas. Discuss safe boundaries and options for resolution.[32]

Ephesians 4:25-27 (NKJV) states,

> Therefore, putting away lying, "Let each one of *you speak truth with his neighbor*," for we are members of one another. "Be angry, and do not sin": do not let the sun go down on your wrath, nor give place to the devil."

The Lord did intend for us as His people to resolve issues in a Christ-like manner. I will leave you with this thought. This is a quote from one of our friends.

> "We are not perfect, but parts of us are excellent."

We would all benefit greatly if we focused on the excellent parts!

Foundational Stone Twelve

> Praise him with the clash of cymbals, praise him with resounding cymbals.
>
> Psalm 150:5 (NIV)

Remember, when cymbals are brought together at the appropriate time during a concert, they add a beautiful climax to the symphony being played. Let us make a symphony together with our words to one another that build up and never tear down.

We will resolve conflict in the following ways:

_____

_____

_____

_____

_____

_____

_____

_____

Foundational Stone Thirteen

We will speak the truth in love in the following ways:

Foundational Stone Fourteen

We will not go to bed angry with one another because:

_____

_____

_____

_____

_____

_____

_____

_____

_____

_____

The Piggy Bank

> For which one of you, when he wants to build a tower, does not first sit down and calculate the cost to see if he has enough to complete it? Otherwise, when he has laid a foundation and is not able to finish, all who observe it begin to ridicule him, saying, "This man began to build and was not able to finish."
>
> Luke 14:28-30 (NIV)

All of us at one time or another has had a bank sitting on our dresser in our bedroom. For a great deal of us, the bank has been in a shape of a pig! One of my granddaughters has a piggy bank; the other one has a princess bank. I was thinking how on earth a piggy bank ever came into being. Of all the places you could throw your loose change, why a pig? Pigs have been the cliché for many sentences I have used when speaking to my daughters growing up in an attempt to bring awareness of their dirtiness. As toddlers I might say, "You look like a dirty little pig who has been rolling in the mud," or "Look at that piggy face." As the girls grew older I would exclaim, "Your room looks like a pigsty." Seems to me pigs just do not have a lot of purpose other than for bacon. The thought of saving money and pigs just does not go together. I did some research to discover how piggy banks were invented. Many inventions evolve simply by accident, and the piggy bank was one of those. Considering the millions of dollars that have been made selling piggy banks, I wish I was the one who had thought of it.

To my amazement, there are many websites in reference to piggy banks, and people even collect them. In the fifteenth century, metal was seldom used for pots and pans due to the cost of metal. Inexpensive clay was used to make dishes, pots, and pans, and this clay was called *pygg*. Housewives would often throw change into a clay jar in efforts to save extra money, and they called it their *pygg* bank. As the years passed by and women continued to call this jar their *pygg bank*, it was forgotten that *pygg* was in reference to the clay that the jar was made out of.

Years later, around the eighteenth or nineteenth century, craftsmen were asked to make *pygg* banks. Unaware, they fashioned these banks into pigs. This was a great hit with the housewives as well as with the children; hence, the piggy bank.[33]

Unfortunately, many couples enter into marriage with a piggy bank mentality; it will all work out, and they do not form a structure for their finances. The piggy bank is their only form of saving. Even marriages with twenty years under their belt squeak by through life with the piggy bank mentality, living paycheck to paycheck, and have little hope for change. People even take money out of their children's piggy banks to pay for something (I admit I did this once to pay for a pizza before debit cards were around). When thinking in regard to the princess bank, at least we are starting off with more of a royalty mentality; after all, we are called a royal priesthood in 1 Peter 2:9. The Bible has much to say when it comes to money and finances. As couples we would be wise to apply these principles, setting in place another great foundational stone.

Earlier in this manual, we made mention of God being a God of covenant. A covenant is a permanent arrangement of a promise by God and an obligation of terms to be fulfilled by His people. His people fulfill their part willingly and benefit greatly by God's promise, which is always for their good. Throughout Scripture, these covenants have been declared by God. The word *covenant* occurs two hundred and eighty times in the Bible. The blessing for obedience and the curse for disobedience has been established by God if we obey or disobey. In Scripture, God has declared He is bound by His Word: "My covenant I will not break, nor alter the word that has gone out of My lips" (Psalm 89:34, NKJV). The CEV says, "I won't break my agreement or go back on my word." In Isaiah 40:8 (NKJV) we are reminded, "The grass withers, the flower fades, but the word of our God stands forever." When it comes to finance and marriage, you have heard it before, but we must state it again. There is a covenant that God has mandated; when we as couples fulfill our part, we are guaranteed God will honor His Word to us. The principle of the tithe cannot be understated. If you want the financial aspect of your marriage to go well, you must adhere to the tithe. As a believer, the best financial plan set in place without the tithe will not allow God's best to be fulfilled in your marriage and family.

Study the following scripture in reference to the tithe:

> For I the *Lord do not change*; therefore you, O children of Jacob, are not consumed. From the days of your fathers you have turned aside from my statutes and have not kept them. *Return to me, and I will return to you*, says the Lord of hosts. But you say, "How shall we return?" Will man rob God? *Yet you are robbing me*. But you say, "How have we robbed you?" *In your tithes and contributions. You are cursed with a curse, for you are robbing me*, the whole

We Promise

nation of you. *Bring the full tithes into the storehouse*, that there may be food in my house. And thereby put me to the test, says the Lord of hosts, *if I will not open the windows of heaven for you and pour down for you a blessing until there is no more need. I will rebuke the devourer for you, so that it will not destroy the fruits of your soil, and your vine in the field shall not fail to bear, says the Lord of hosts.* Then all nations will call you blessed, for you will be a land of delight, says the Lord of hosts.

Malachi 3:6-12 (ESV)

Does the Lord change?

_____

If we return to the covenant God has established, what does He promise to do?

_____

How do we rob God?

_____

If we do not tithe, what does the Bible say we are under?

_____

What do you think a curse is, and how can this affect your life, marriage, and family members?

_____

What do you think a tithe is?

_____

What do you think an offering or contribution is?

_____

Are we ever to test God?

_____

If we bring the tithe and offerings to God, what does He say He will do?

_____

_____

Re-read Malachi 3:6-12 in *The Message* version for clearer understanding.

I have heard many people say that tithing is Old Testament and does not apply to us today. The following few verses should bring clarity to the tithe and the New Testament, with additional study there are also other verses to support this.

- Matthew 23:23
- Luke 11:42
- Matthew 8:3-4
- Luke 18:12
- Hebrews 7:4-9

I wish we as a couple had instituted the tithe principle into our marriage right from the get-go. I am very thankful eventually we did and were able to instill this principle into our daughters' lives. The Lord proved Himself mighty several years ago in the life of one of our daughters. She had always been a tither, even as a young girl. Our daughter is also very mindful of saving money. She has no problem spending other's money but does not want to spend her own money. When she was four years old, she had a piggy bank full of money. Her father wanted to trade her a twenty-dollar bill for her twenty one-dollar bills. The exchange was made; however, about ten minutes later after she had given this great thought, she had a meltdown, crying and accusing her dad of stealing all her money. One day when she was home from college, she was sporting a new leather coat. She asked her dad how he liked the coat. His reply was he really liked it, very sharp. She then went on to proclaim, "Good, I am glad you like it, because you paid for it."

Unfortunately, when she was twenty-three, she went through a very tragic situation. This was the darkest night our daughter had ever experienced. The effects of this situation were far-reaching, and every member of our family was affected in one way or another. For Dan and me as a couple, it was our darkest night also. The heart-wrenching pain was the greatest we ever endured, and most of the time we felt completely helpless toward what was happening with our daughter. We fought through every emotion from denial, anger, helplessness, to a fight of determination, and forgiveness. Whenever we were unsure of what to do next, the Lord moved swiftly to order our steps and direct us. God orchestrated divine appointments at critical moments and made sure the right decisions were made. Because of all that took place, our daughter was left with credit card debt (not her own) as well as a house mortgage that she was responsible for.

God proved Himself mighty; the Lord became Isaiah 54:2-6 in her life as well as Malachi 3:10-12. Nothing is more heart-wrenching than for a parent to watch one of their children be wounded in body, soul, mind, and spirit as well as financially. We encouraged our daughter to continue to tithe, even though her financial expenses were much greater than her income. Within a few months she was given a 14 percent raise by her employer. She is now twenty-seven. All credit card debt has been paid off. She has a large sum in her IRA, and she just paid cash for a 2009 Chevy Cobalt. The Lord has granted her great favor with her employer, and she has been awarded several promotions. A wonderful man has come into her life to be her husband, and she is still a princess after midnight! Within eight months of marriage, our daughter and her husband paid cash for a fully loaded 2008 Ford Edge in mint condition with a blue book value of $24,000.

I want to be very frank. Our daughter's story is one of triumph over tragedy, which financially speaking was resolved in a fast time period. I realize there are many stories of faithful tithing believers who are sustained and faithful to the tithe while waiting for resolution. I believe being sustained is also a miracle. I cannot help but think of the story of Joseph in Genesis 37-39. This story has a time span of approximately twenty-two years. There are times I think Dan and I can really relate to this story. In October of 2008, we were headed for a conference in Orlando, Florida, with the National Christian Counseling Association, which my husband is a member of (Dan worked a secular job while serving in ministry on a part-time basis).

On the way to the airport we got a call from one of our daughters saying it was on the news; his place of employment was closing. This came as a huge shock and one we were totally unprepared for. We discussed if we should cancel the trip even though there would be no refund for the conference fees or air flight. If we canceled, at least we could save on hotel fees as well as food. After a long discussion, we decided the Lord knew all this ahead of time, and we should continue on. Our faith as a couple had been stretched in a way as never before. Fortunately, we have always had a good, steady income. We had a tentative strategy in place for when Dan should retire, and that plan was about ten years down the road. The plan also included how we would become debt-free with no home mortgages. I would never suggest anyone do this, but in 2001 we purchased a small cottage without selling our main house. Our intent was that we would sell the house we raised our daughters in and live in the cottage, since there was just the two of us. To make a long story short, nine years later we still have the house because it never sold.

Fast forward; so here we are in 2010 with two houses, and my husband no longer employed by his employer of thirty-three years. I guess you could say we now work for the King. Words could never describe my gratitude and thanksgiving to the King of kings and the Lord of lords who truly is faithful to His everlasting Word. The Lord continues to sustain us each month with two house mortgages and the expense of owning two homes. I wish I could tell you I have gone through this process gracefully. I have fought against fear and worry, creating the need to constantly put them in their place, reminding myself of God's Word and His unrelenting faithfulness to us through the years. Little did I know that before 2010 would come to an end and before *We Promise* would make it to print, the Lord would send a buyer for our house of twenty-four years. A very excited young family is now raising their children in the place we had called home.

Eric and Colleen, from the chapter "Honor Guards," have an important story about tithing as well. When Colleen was in the hospital for several months after the stroke, Eric was not able to work. Eric's employment has been a commission-only in pay, and during the time of Colleen's hospitalization, the Lord was faithful to sustain and provide for them financially. Eric and Colleen had always practiced the principle of tithing.

Now that the importance of the tithe has been established, we can move forward and establish other financial principles. I am a firm believer in not re-inventing the wheel. There are great resources out there for establishing good financial principles. Below is a non-inclusive list. We strongly suggest you invest your time into studying what these experts have to say about finance.

- Provident Plan, www.providentplan.com
- Crown Financial Ministries, www.crown.org
- Dave Ramsey—Financial Peace University, www.daveramsey.com
- Christian Personal Finance, www.christianpf.com

When developing a spending blueprint, issues of the heart need to be examined in how money is viewed. We can all agree on one thing; we need money to live. How we view money can have a dynamic effect on our spending habits as man and wife.[34]

- How can we establish contentment in our life? Read 1 Timothy 6:6 and Philippians 4:11-13

  _____

- Do we exhibit self-control, and how do we express this? Read Galatians 5:22-23 and 1 Thessalonians 5:4-8

  _____

- Are we selfish or selfless? Read 1 Corinthians 10:24

  _____

- Do we rejoice with others or become envious? Read James 3:14-16

  _____

- Where is our security found? Read Ecclesiastes and 1 Timothy 6:17-19

  _____

- Do we feel we are entitled to something? Does someone owe us? Do we long for what someone else has? Read Genesis 3:2-6, Exodus 20:17, and Colossians 3:5

  _____

- Do we allow our emotions to rule us? Do we spend money on things we cannot afford? Are we willing to do whatever it takes to get these wants and desires, regardless of the cost? Read Matthew 6:1-20, 24, 1 Peter 2:11, Mark 7:23, Proverbs 16:8, and 2 Corinthians 8:1-5

  _____

In the end we will not be taking a U-Haul to heaven with us. Keeping our hearts and perspectives in the right place when it comes to money will be of great help as we develop the spending plan, or what is called a budget.

Preparing a Budget

Income

Husband's monthly take-home pay

_____

Wife's monthly take-home pay

_____

Other monthly income

_____

Expense

Tithe (10% of total monthly gross income)

_____

Savings (IRAs, general saving account)

_____

Mortgage or rent (20%)

_____

Home maintenance (10% of mortgage)

_____

Utilities (gas, electric, water, garbage, phone, cable) (12%)

_____

Groceries (8%)

_____

Eating out (3%)

_____

Vehicles (car payments, gas, insurance, repairs, maintenance) (14%)

_____

Healthcare (medical, dental, eye, prescriptions, co-pays) (6%)

_____

Clothing (4%)

_____

Entertainment (3%)

_____

Personal care (toiletries, hair, make-up, etc.) (2%)

_____

Insurance (health, life, other) (10%)

_____

Special occasions (birthday, Christmas, Valentine's Day, etc.)

_____

Child care

_____

Remember, work is not a dirty four-letter word. What do the following scriptures have to say about working? Read 2 Thessalonians 3:10,12 and Proverbs 30:25.

_____

_____

The following is a list of a *few* scriptures for your information in regard to the different aspects of finance. The websites mentioned earlier in this chapter will be valuable resources for you as you learn about finance and make application for your marriage and family.

- Deuteronomy 28:43-45
- Proverbs 22:7
- Isaiah 24:2
- Exodus 22:25
- Deuteronomy 15:6
- Psalm 112:5
- Ezekiel 18:7
- Habakkuk 2:6-7
- Luke 6:34-35
- Proverbs 28:8
- Proverbs 3:27-28
- Matthew 5:25-26
- Romans 13:8
- Colossians 2:14

Foundational Stone Fifteen

Our goal for finances in the year is: Insert your financial budget here, along with any other financial goals you would like to achieve (this budget may need to be revised yearly or more often if financial income changes or expenses change):

_____

_____

_____

_____

_____

_____

_____

_____

_____

_____

A Loyal Heart and a Willing Mind

> As for you, my son Solomon, know the God of your father, and serve Him with a loyal heart and with a willing mind; for the LORD searches all hearts and understands all the intent of the thoughts. If you seek Him, He will be found by you; but if you forsake Him, He will cast you off forever.
>
> 1 Chronicles 28:9 (NKJV)

Just as Jesus did when he created wine out of water and it was said, "But you have saved the best till now" (John 2:10, NIV), I believe I have saved the best for last. In this last chapter we will cover three foundational stones, deepening our spiritual walk with the Lord, serving and worshiping together, and training our children spiritually. Volumes of books could be written and are already in print covering the spiritual aspect of marriage and the dynamical importance of establishing this in marriage. For the sake of length, I will only be able to scratch the surface on this subject.

Deepening Our Spiritual Walk

Prayer has been my solace. I recall countless times during my childhood years kneeling at my bedside, pouring my heart out to Jesus. I carried this prayer life into our marriage. I cannot imagine where, what, when, or how our marriage would have transpired, survived, or flourished without the power of prayer. We have had the privilege of being the recipients of countless answered prayers. There have been many benchmarks and turning points in our lives through the power of answered prayer. I am eternally grateful to our heavenly Father, who continues to answer prayer daily, and even answers the prayers I have forgotten I had prayed. I have also witnessed the power of answered prayer in the lives of others. I served on the leadership team of Healing Rooms of Grand Rapids for over six years. Healing Rooms is a ministry that serves others through the power of prayer and the laying on of hands. I, as well as other team members, prayed for thousands of people who were sick in body or mind. I witnessed countless people receive healing in their body. I was also able to see those who were in bondage set free, as well as mental illness healed.

Great miracles have taken place at Healing Rooms and at the conferences we sponsored. Some of the healings I witnessed were deaf ears healed, scoliosis healed, PTS (Post Traumatic Stress Syndrome) healed, backs healed, knees healed, diabetes healed, eyes healed, chronic depression set free, bipolar set free, barrenness set free, stomach issues healed, brain cancer healed, and the list goes on. In the six years I served at Healing Rooms, we had a large filing cabinet full of files testifying to answered prayer and healing of bodies as well as deliverance from bondages. Words of knowledge and hope were given out to those who were desperately seeking God for hope and direction. I am amazed that the Lord cares so much for His children that He would trust and use me to deliver a message to one of His children. People are blown away when God gives me a word of knowledge just for them (through listening prayer), something I had no way of possibly knowing. God knows, and He wants His child to know He is thinking of them.

One of the most bizarre things that I have ever done was deliver a word to a woman from the Lord. I remember arguing with God. "Oh, no, Lord, I could not possibly have heard you correctly. This woman will think I am totally nuts if I tell her that." As I looked at her I saw a cheese curl in her hair (bizarre, I told you). The Lord impressed upon me to tell her that she was just like a cheese curl; He just could not get enough of her, and on it went. I waited listening to God hoping that I was way off; however, God kept prodding me, so I went for it and told her exactly that. Well, to my amazement, this woman came to me later with bubbling joy dancing all over her. She went on to explain that she loved cheese curls and would mail them all over the country to her friends! She couldn't wait to share this with all her friends. God loves that cheesy curl lady and must get a kick out of her sending cheesy curls all over the country. That woman was so touched, because God showed up that day and gave her a great big kiss. I must admit after this happened, I am a little more confident to speak when the Lord is prompting me to share with one of His children.

Today I believe the older generation is feeling misplaced and that God does not have a plan to use them any longer. I think there is disrespect going on for the older, seasoned believers, or even older people in general. This is quite evident even in the work force where the older employee with the knowledge and experience is being replaced with someone younger, and these older individuals cannot find a job, even if they are overqualified for it. I have a heart for the older saints of God who have paved the way, and we still need them. My heart as a young girl and woman was touched and impacted by the influence of the older saints of God.

One day I was serving at Healing Rooms, and an older man came in. He wanted prayer. He felt his life was used up and God had no purpose for him anymore. He wanted to still serve God; but he felt his day was done. We went to prayer. The Lord dropped something in my mind; once again I was hesitant to speak, but the prodding of God was strong. I began to share with this old saint of God that the Lord sees him as a pony express rider. I continued to elaborate as I felt the Lord moving me. When I had finished, the man began to share with me that he was a truck driver who had a routine route; he enjoyed sharing Jesus wherever he went on this route. This man also began to share that in his family line was a history of circuit riders. Circuit riders were like pony express riders, but instead of delivering mail, they delivered the Word of God on the circuit they rode. Yes, once again the Lord showed up and gave this old saint of God a great big kiss and let him know He still had a plan to use him. God is on the move, and so is the power of His Word to do exactly what He says it will do. Prayer is a tool to unleash the unprecedented power of the God most high. I strongly believe in the power of prayer. Prayer has been the catalyst in my life that has taken me into a deeper more intimate relationship with the Father.

Developing an intimate individual prayer life is important, but equally important is learning to pray together and being comfortable with each other's style of praying. From the Bible we learn there is added benefit as we pray together. The important key is to just do it. The more you pray together, the more comfortable you will become, and it will also lead to a more intimate relationship as a couple. Study the following scriptures and learn the dynamics of praying together.

> Again I say to you that if two of you agree on earth concerning anything that they ask, it will be done for them by My Father in heaven. For where two or three are gathered together in My name, I am there in the midst of them.
> Matthew 18:19-20 (NKJV)

> These all continued with one accord in prayer and supplication, with the women and Mary the mother of Jesus, and with His brothers.
> Acts 1:14 (NKJV)

Read Acts 12:1-19.

The Lord has given us as believers the power to overcome evil, to build up and spur one another on to greatness and victory! We do not have to walk around hopeless, but hopeful. We are His royal priesthood. Know who you are and the authority you have in Jesus. Prayer will not only loose heaven's provision in your life and marriage, it will loose heaven's abundance into your life and marriage. In Matthew 11:12 (NKJV) it says, "And from the days of John the Baptist until now the kingdom of heaven suffers violence, and the violent take it by force." The definition of *violent*[35] is: "physical force or activity used to cause harm, damage, or abuse, exhibiting intense emotional or mental excitement: passionate intensity, *heat*." The definition of *force* is: "to compel to do something or to act, to obtain by coercion; to bring forth, as with effort; to move or drive against resistance; to break down by force; to press or impose; as one's will. Strong, effective, powerful, vigorous."

> The kingdom of heaven, which Jesus set up as a powerful movement or reign among men suffers violence, requires of them an equally strong and radical reaction. The violent then who take it by force are people of keen enthusiasm and commitment who are willing to respond to and propagate with radical abandonment the message and dynamic of God's reign.[36]

Jesus was passionate about prayer, and this is evident when we read Hebrews 5:7-8 (NKJV):

> Who, in the days of His flesh, when He had offered up prayers and supplications, *with vehement cries and tears* to Him who was able to save Him from death, and was heard because of His godly fear, though He was a Son, yet He learned obedience by the things which He suffered.

Christ's passion is also displayed in John 11:33-36 (NKJV):

> Therefore, when Jesus saw her weeping, and the Jews who came with her weeping, *He groaned in the spirit and was troubled*. And He said, "Where have you laid him?" They said to Him, "Lord, come and see." *Jesus wept*. Then the Jews said, "See how He loved him!"

To understand the intensity of the words *groaned* and *wept*, or *vehement cries* and *tears*, further definition is required. *Groaned*: "to snort with anger, murmur against, to utter a deep prolonged sound of disapproval." *Wept*: "wail out load, mourn." *Vehement*: "boisterous, mighty, violent, forcibly uttered, powerful." *Cries*: "outcry, clamour, tumult, grief."[37]

We Promise

> In His plan of salvation for humankind God has ordained that believers be co-workers with Him. In some respects God has limited himself to the holy, believing, preserving prayers of his people. Think of Prayer: violence that can explode the impossible!
>
> Jack Hayford

"Prayerlessness is the most prohibitive obstacle in the road to a believer's victory, no matter what our specific pursuit may be" (Author unknown). Prayer without faith is like a ball without a bat. The Word of God says in Hebrews 11:6, "But without faith *it is* impossible to please *Him*, for he who comes to God must believe that He is, and *that* He is a rewarder of those who diligently seek Him." Think of prayer as the *ball* and the *bat* as faith. The bat of faith hits the ball of prayer out of the park for a home run! Looking at Mark 11:20-25 (NKJV), it says,

> Now in the morning, as they passed by, they saw the fig tree dried up from the roots. And Peter, remembering, said to Him, "Rabbi, look! The fig tree which You cursed has withered away." So Jesus answered and said to them, "*Have faith in God. For assuredly, I say to you, whoever says to this mountain, 'Be removed and be cast into the sea,' and does not doubt in his heart, but believes that those things he says will be done, he will have whatever he says.* Therefore I say to you, whatever things you ask when you pray, *believe that you receive them, and you will have them.* And whenever you stand praying, if you have anything against anyone, forgive him, that your Father in heaven may also forgive you your trespasses. But if you do not forgive, neither will your Father in heaven forgive your trespasses."

Notice at the end of verse 25 there is a condition that must be fulfilled: *forgiveness*. We discussed forgiveness in the chapter "Clashing Cymbals." In James 1:6-8 (NKJV), it says, "But let him ask in faith, with no doubting, for he who doubts is like a wave of the sea driven and tossed by the wind. For let not that man suppose that he will receive anything from the Lord; he is a double-minded man, unstable in all his ways." I don't know about you, but I for one don't want to be a double-minded man. I truly desire my prayers to be answered. I want my faith to be stable and sure, not wavering. This faith can only be developed through relationship with the Father. Our history with God shapes our faith.

I had one of those moments in the physical a few years ago that created a great teaching parable; I believe if you stretch your thinking process you can relate this spiritually to yourself. This lesson not only taught me a physical lesson, but it really made me take a look at my faith level.

I was leaving for a jobsite in Battle Creek. I had been there several times before. I did not take my MapQuest map, and my GPS was in my glove compartment. I bought it after a trip to Chicago. Although I had my MapQuest map with me in Chicago, there were five lanes of one-way traffic; I had to yield right but was uncertain which right lane to get into so I could get off on the appropriate exit. You guessed it; I chose the wrong lane and was dumped off on a one-way street, not even sure how to get back on the highway because of the one-way roads. I was now in downtown Chicago; I was smart enough to stop and ask for directions immediately (I really prayed God would put the right person before me); yes, they gave me great directions, and I arrived at my destination. When I returned home I bought the GPS, determined if I used it, I would get my verbal warning, and it would tell me the exact lane I need the next time.

To make a long story short, I hate my GPS system because I cannot see the entire journey all the way to my destination before my eyes. So I am back to using MapQuest. Now back to the Battle Creek story. I took off without MapQuest and did not plug in the GPS. I knew there was one turn I did not want to miss, or I would end up in the wrong section of Battle Creek. You guessed it. I took a wrong turn; well, I did not take the time to plug in my GPS, nor did I stop and ask for directions. I kept driving, hoping I would find my way there. Eventually I did; I knew if I could see a sign for the hospital and follow that, the office where my job was, was directly across the street.

The Lord began to use this physical lesson and apply it to my spiritual walk. One of my old pastors used to say, "For everything in the physical, there is a spiritual ramification." I believe he was right. God speaks to us in all types of ways. He constantly desires to teach us if we will take the time to learn. We just need to plug into His *GPS—God's Positioning System.*

Let me drive this point home further. I think there are three types of people when it comes to faith.

- Winging Its (those who wing it through life)
- Maps (Man's Attempts, Plans, and Strategies)
- GPS (God's Positioning System)

We all start out with the same faith in the same place at salvation; however, after that, we all take our own distinct faith walk in life. How do we determine what we're going to do with this thing called faith? How are we going to get directions for each day, month, or year? Some of us will stay stuck as Winging Its. Others will soar right past Winging It and Maps and apply

GPS to our lives. Others will flop back and forth, visiting each level frequently. Now we will unpack this and see if we can find some answers.

Visualize your life as a car, the car representing your life.

Winging Its: These are people who go through life knowing their salvation but take little time to develop any faith. They get in their car called life thinking, I am pretty sure I know how to get where I am going; I'll just stop for directions (not!) and ask if I get lost. The Wing It's car may be a small four-cylinder economy car, a hand-me-down from Grandma who only put 25,000 miles on it during her ownership. The car looks nice, spotless when it was given, and does fifty-five miles per hour on a good day. Of course there definitely is not enough horsepower to pass anyone, and how could it? Other cars pass by like the car is standing still. They have a great car that's in great shape, but no Holy Ghost power to direct and drive them. They have failed to fuel the tank and boost the engine with the discipline and direction of the Word of God. They just want to wing it! Their faith is like *foxhole* faith: they call on the Lord when they're really in trouble or in over their head.

Man's Attempts, Plans, and Strategies: I am self-employed, and I am an adamant user of MapQuest. I never try to leave for a job site without MapQuest in hand. You type in your beginning and end destination, and the whole journey is mapped out for you! Every step of the journey with exact mileage is at your fingertips. There is no guessing where your next turn will be; it is laid out before your eyes, every mile of the journey. You feel confident that you will arrive at your destination unharmed, unscathed, and right on time. No detours are planned in your fully equipped V-6 mid-size sedan. This car called life has some gusto and goes through the journey pretty well until the detours come, black ice suddenly appears, and an unexpected flat tire delays the journey. You are unprepared for the trial and tribulations of life; in James 1:2-8 NIV it says:

> Consider it pure joy, my brothers, whenever you face trials of many kinds, because you know that the testing of your faith develops perseverance. Perseverance must finish its work so that you may be mature and complete, not lacking anything. If any of you lacks wisdom, he should ask God, who gives generously to all without finding fault, and it will be given to him. But when he asks, he must believe and not doubt, because he who doubts is like a wave of the sea, blown and tossed by the wind. That man should not think he will receive anything from the Lord; he is a double-minded man, unstable in all he does.

Your car is fully loaded, but because you must know the entire journey before you start, the unexpected suddenly throws you and frustrates you. You begin to doubt because you thought you were prepared, you thought you knew the best way to arrive at your destination, but now the journey has changed, and it shakes you. Your faith seems great as long as things go as planned. But put the detour in there, and now you question your faith and your God.

GPS (God's Positioning System): It takes a mature faith to depend and lean on GPS. First you must pause before you take off in your fully loaded limited edition V-8 luxury SUV with so many bells and whistles you do not know how to use them all. You must take the time to read the owner's manual (the Bible), but not just read it; study it so you do not forget how to utilize all the benefits of this marvelous vehicle and all its features. In addition to every extra you could possibly want, this SUV comes with a built-in GPS system; you don't even have to plug it into the lighter; however, you still must take the time to pause and program it (pray). Then you must wait for the first direction to announce itself. As you start out on your journey, you have faith that when the next turn is about to come, you will have a warning. But if the radio is blasting, you are on your cell phone, and other distractions are coming at you, it is possible that you will miss the voice that says in five hundred feet to turn left. You may run into an unexpected detour, but with GPS you can pause and ask for an alternate route (pray)! You will not be shaken, because you know if you ask you will receive. Matthew 7:7 (NIV), "Ask and it will be given to you; seek and you will find; knock and the door will be opened to you."

In your spiritual walk, you must keep your ears tuned to the voice of the Holy Spirit. When we walk or drive through this journey called life, being fully equipped prevents those detours from shaking us.

"*If you remain in me and my words remain in you*, ask whatever you wish, and it will be given you" (John 15:7, NIV). Once again, faith is the bat that hits the ball of prayer out of the park for a home run!

Worshiping and Serving Together

Worshiping and serving together is a theme that is carried throughout the New Testament as well as the Old Testament. God's people were meant to fellowship together. There are countless stories throughout the Bible of what God's people were able to accomplish when they stayed in unity. Hebrews 10:23-25 (NKJV) says,

> Let us hold fast the confession of *our* hope without wavering, for He who promised *is* faithful. And let us consider one another in order to stir up love and good works, not forsaking the assembling of ourselves together, as *is* the

> manner of some, but exhorting *one another,* and so much the more as you see the Day approaching.

What are the themes in the following verses, and how would you apply this as a couple? Read Hebrews 3:3, Acts 2:42-47, Hebrews 6:1-3, 1 Corinthians 12:12-31, Psalm 22:3, 2 Chronicles 20:15-30, and Joshua 6.

_____

_____

_____

_____

I have read countless times that 10 percent of the people in churches do 100 percent of the work. Dan and I have served in the churches we have attended in various aspects. Different seasons of our lives have determined to what extent we have been able to serve. During the child-rearing years, what our children were involved in normally dictated how we were serving. When they were babies we served in the nursery; as they grew, we taught Sunday school. During the junior high and high school years we were youth leaders and chaperoned many of the youth activities. Even though we were very active in our children's lives, we attended small groups so we could stay connected and fellowship with others our own age.

Something that I struggled with greatly was being envious of other women who were very involved with ministry. I had a strong passion to participate at a deeper level in ministry, but my passion for being a wife and mother overruled this. I felt I had to set that passion aside for another season of my life. I did participate in going to women's Bible studies and attended a women's retreat once a year; beyond that I felt my focus needed to be with my family and their spiritual needs. Once my children had left home, with my husband's blessing, I was able to pursue ministry. For over six years, I served on the leadership team of Healing Rooms of Grand Rapids. This was an incredible time of not only serving but learning as well. Toward the end of those six years I felt the Lord drawing me away and knew I was to serve alongside of my husband. We now oversee the pre-marriage counseling program as well as the Marriage Mentor Program at our church. We also founded Light Dawns Ministries, which is a pastoral biblical counseling ministry. Serving together is a longing fulfilled in us as a couple. We desired to serve the Lord together for years, but the Lord knew what season was best for us. Proverbs 13:12 (NIV) states, "Hope deferred makes the heart sick, but a longing fulfilled is a tree of life."

We always encourage couples to find a way to serve the Lord together in their local church or another ministry. This does not have to entail hours each week. It could be one hour a week or two to three hours a month. Serving together brings couples closer and creates a more intimate relationship with one another as well as with the Lord. When considering how or what you will do, we encourage you to take into consideration each other's temperaments. If one person is outgoing but the other is not, you must find something that suits you both well. For instance, say one person is outgoing and the other is not. You could serve at your church's coffee shop. The outgoing person could take the order; the introverted person could make the coffee. The point is you're together doing something for the Lord. If that is not spiritual enough for you, try hosting a small group. The outgoing person could lead the study; the introverted person could make food or prepare the music. I think you get the general idea.

Discovering how you would like to serve as a couple could be a fun date night, granting much conversation. You may have to try a few things and see what fits well for you. Examine what you are passionate about individually and as a couple when it comes to serving. Remember, we all go through seasons of life, and serving in ministry will change with your seasons as a family.

Raising Our Children for the Lord

As parents, we are responsible not only for taking care of our children's physical and emotional needs, we have also been given charge to train them spiritually. The Bible is very clear we are the ones to train our children in Him. Whether or not you have children, this area must be discussed, and as parents we need to be in agreement with how we will train our children. It is very confusing and unsettling for children whose parents undermine each other and have not established clear agreeable guidelines in reference to children.

Let's take a look at a few scriptures in regard to children.

> So they said, "Believe on the Lord Jesus Christ, and you will be saved, you and your household." Then they spoke the word of the Lord to him and to all who were in his house. And he took them the same hour of the night and washed *their* stripes. And immediately he and all his family were baptized.

Now when he had brought them into his house, he set food before them; and he rejoiced, having believed in God with all his household.

Acts 16:31 (NKJV)

Those who are planted in the house of the Lord shall flourish in the courts of our God. They shall still bear fruit in old age; they shall be fresh and flourishing, to declare that the Lord is upright; *He is* my rock, and *there is* no unrighteousness in Him.

Psalm 92:13-15 (NKJV)

Train up a child in the way he should go, and when he is old he will not depart from it.

Proverbs 22:6 (NKJV)

Only take heed to yourself, and diligently keep yourself, lest you forget the things your eyes have seen, and lest they depart from your heart all the days of your life. And teach them to your children and your grandchildren, *especially concerning* the day you stood before the Lord your God in Horeb, when the Lord said to me, "Gather the people to Me, and I will let them hear My words, that they may learn to fear Me all the days they live on the earth, and *that* they may teach their children."

Deuteronomy 4: 9-10 (NKJV)

And these words which I command you today shall be in your heart. You shall teach them diligently to your children, and shall talk of them when you sit in your house, when you walk by the way, when you lie down, and when you rise up. You shall bind them as a sign on your hand, and they shall be as frontlets between your eyes. You shall write them on the doorposts of your house and on your gates.

Deuteronomy 6:7-9 (NKJV)

Now therefore, fear the Lord, serve Him in sincerity and in truth, and put away the gods which your fathers served on the other side of the River and in Egypt. Serve the Lord! And if it seems evil to you to serve the Lord, choose for yourselves this day whom you will serve, whether the gods which your fathers served that *were* on the other side of the River, or the gods of the Amorites, in whose land you dwell. But as for me and my house, we will serve the Lord.

Joshua 24:14-15 (NKJV)

Here are a few other scriptures for you to look up on your own:
- Proverbs 12:1
- Proverbs 13:1,18,24
- Proverbs 15:5,10,32
- Proverbs 19:18
- Proverbs 22:15
- Proverbs 23:13-14
- Hebrews 12:7-11
- Psalm 127
- Isaiah 49:23-26 (my favorite)
- Isaiah 54:13

We suggest the following books as resource material for raising children:
Shepherding a Child's Heart by Tedd Tripp

Books by Dr. James Dobson:

Dare to Discipline

Bringing Up Girls

Bringing Up Boys

The Strong-Willed Child

Preparing for Adolescence

Parenting Isn't for Cowards

Raising children is certainly as rewarding as it is challenging. I believe after you have raised your children is when you are really ready to raise your children! We all wish we could change the hand of time on some things. Unfortunately, we are only given one time around. With today's resources available to us at a click of a mouse, we should be able to reap from others who have gone before us. Our parents and grandparents can be one of the best resources available to draw insight from when it comes to rearing children. Being in unity as a couple will reap great rewards in the lives of your children.

The last three foundational stones are now ready to be laid.

Foundational Stone Sixteen

But as for me and my house, we will serve the Lord.

Joshua 24:15b (NKJV)

*We will deepen our spiritual walk with the Lord by _____
and desire to serve the Lord together in the following ways:*

_____

_____

_____

_____

_____

_____

_____

_____

_____

Foundational Stone Seventeen

We will not forsake the assembly of the saints (Hebrews 10:25); we will surround ourselves by other believers in the following ways:

_____

_____

_____

_____

_____

_____

_____

_____

_____

Foundational Stone Eighteen

Together we will raise our children in the Lord in the following ways:

_____

_____

_____

_____

_____

_____

_____

_____

_____

_____

_____

_____

Conclusion

Jesus said a prayer to the Father prior to His betrayal, arrest, crucifixion, and resurrection. This prayer is for all believers. When I studied this prayer and the impact of the words Jesus spoke, I could not help but think of the dynamic impact this will have on marriage. What better place of oneness should this prayer and the fulfillment of this prayer be demonstrated?

> I do not pray for these alone, but also for those who will believe in Me through their word; that they all may be one, as You, Father, *are* in Me, and I in You; that they also may be one in Us, that the world may believe that You sent Me. And the glory which You gave Me I have given them, that they may be one just as We are one: I in them, and You in Me; that they may be made perfect in one, and that the world may know that You have sent Me, and have loved them as You have loved Me. "Father, I desire that they also whom You gave Me may be with Me where I am, that they may behold My glory which You have given Me; for You loved Me before the foundation of the world. O righteous Father! The world has not known You, but I have known You; and these have known that You sent Me. And I have declared to them Your name, and will declare *it,* that the love with which You loved Me may be in them, and I in them."
>
> John 17:20-26 (NKJV)

One of the greatest steps has been taken on this lifetime journey of marriage. A covenant has been made to one another. This covenant is a sign, a reminder of an undying promise that you have pledged to one another. The majority of this covenant will remain intact and unchangeable. Some parts such as finance will need to be revisited, to adjust with the season of life you are in. Now that your foundation is set, your future together is filled with God's promises of enjoying a piece of heaven on earth as husband and wife.

We are honored you brought us into your life for this incredible adventure of promise. We would love to hear from you and how *We Promise* has impacted your life. Please write us at: ldm.wepromise@gmail.com

We are available for seminars, special engagement speaking, marriage retreats, and implementing the We Promise *program in your local church or organization. Please email or call for additional information.*

    ldm.wepromise@gmail.com
    www.lightdawns.org
    www.pennypoints.blogspot.com
    In honor of marriage,
    Dan and Penny Loosenort

Note to Leaders

If you are intending on using this manual to teach a pre-marriage or marriage class, your leader's manual is this manual after you have completed it yourselves. Completing this manual along with your life experience should adequately prepare you to teach this manual.

Recommended Resources

Listed are a few resources (some of my favorite) that you may find beneficial:

Marriage Today, http://www.marriagetoday.org

Family Life, http://www.familylife.com

Focus on the Family, http://www.focusonthefamily.com

Bible online, http://www.biblegateway.com

Winning at Home, http://www.winningathome.com/h/

Abigail's (Domestic Violence), http://abigails.org/

Setting the Captives Free, http://www.settingcaptivesfree.com/

Endnotes

1. Harav Yitzchak Ginsburgh, "The Number 18"., *Gal Einai Institue*: http://www.inner.org/respona/leter1/res.33.htm

2. Ira L. Milligan, *Understanding the Dreams You Dream Volume II*. Shippensburg, PA.: Destiny Image, 2000. 41

3. Webster's Dictionary and Thesaurus. Nichols Publishing Group, 1999. 517.

4. Ed Wheat and Gloria Okes Perkins, *Love Life for Every Married Couple*. Grand Rapids, MI.: Zondervan, 1980. 30.

5. Ed Wheat and Gloria Okes Perkins, *Love Life for Every Married Couple*. Grand Rapids, MI.: Zondervan, 1980. 30.

6. Please note, some of the bullets under the heading of "couple" were adapted from material presented at:

   General Council of Assemblies of God, "Our 16 Fundamental Truths," : http://ag.org/top/beliefs/Statement_of_Fundamental_Truths/sft.pdf

7. Ed Wheat and Gloria Okes Perkins, *Love Life for Every Married Couple*. Grand Rapids, MI.: Zondervan, 1980. 31.

8. Please note: some of the material presented in *The Role of the Husband* was adapted from:

Rob Flood, "What Did Jesus Do," (2006): http://www.familylife.com/site/apps/nlnet/content3.aspx?c=dnJHKLNnFoG&b=3781167&ct=4639671

9   James Strong, S.T.D.,LL.D., *Strong's Exhaustive Concordance of The Bible with Greek and Hebrew Dictionaries.* (Christian Hertiage Publishing Company, Inc., 1988), H5826.

10   James Strong, S.T.D.,LL.D., *Strong's Exhaustive Concordance of The Bible with Greek and Hebrew Dictionaries.* (Christian Hertiage Publishing Company, Inc., 1988), H7287

11   Please note, some of the information about women in the Bible was adapted from material presented in: Edith Dean, *All the Women of the Bible,* Harper and Row, 1955, HarperCollins, 1988.

12   Dr. Richard D. Dobins, "*Career VS Motherhood*"(2000): www.emerge.org

13   Kris Vallotton with Bill Johnson, *The Supernatural Ways of Royalty* (Destiny Image Publishers, Inc., 2006), 17-18.

14   James Strong, S.T.D.,LL.D., *Strong's Exhaustive Concordance of The Bible with Greek and Hebrew Dictionaries.* (Christian Hertiage Publishing Company, Inc., 1988), G5091.

15   Ed Wheat and Gloria Okes Perkins, *Love Life for Every Married Couple.* Grand Rapids, MI.: Zondervan, 1980. 31.

16   Donald C. Stamps, *Standards of Sexual Morality*: The Full Life Study Bible New International Version. Life Publishers International. Zondervan Publishing House, 1992. 1936.

17   Donald C. Stamps, *study note*: The Full Life Study Bible New International Version. Life Publishers International. Zondervan Publishing House, 1992. 177.

18   James Strong, S.T.D.,LL.D., *Strong's Exhaustive Concordance of The Bible with Greek and Hebrew Dictionaries.* (Christian Hertiage Publishing Company, Inc., 1988), G5343.

19   Webster Dictionary and Thesaurus. Nichols Publishing Group, 1999. 507.

20   H.B. London Jr., *Pornography: A Very Real and Troublesome Problem,* http://www.pureintimacy.org/piArticles/A000000511.cfm

21   Please note, some of the suggestions in this list were derived from the following:

Mort Fertel, *Marriage Fitness 4 Steps to Building & Maintaining Phenomenal Love.* MarriageMax, Inc., 2004. 108-111, 158-159.

Stephen Kendrick and Alex Kendrick, *The Love Dare*, B&H Publishing Group, 2008. 206-207

Ed Wheat and Gloria Perkins, "The Power of the Touch" (November 2007): *http://www.familylife.com/site/apps/nlnet/content3.aspx?c=dnJHKLNnFoG&b=3781237&ct=4638409&printmode=1*

22 Jeremy Lelek, *"Passionate Worship In God's Temple~Naked But Not Ashamed"*, http://www.christiancounseling.com

23 James Strong, S.T.D.,LL.D., *Strong's Exhaustive Concordance of The Bible with Greek and Hebrew Dictionaries.* (Christian Hertiage Publishing Company, Inc., 1988), G3107

24 Rev. Dr. Ben Fulayter

25 James Strong, S.T.D.,LL.D., *Strong's Exhaustive Concordance of The Bible with Greek and Hebrew Dictionaries.* (Christian Hertiage Publishing Company, Inc., 1988), G264, H205, H4603, H898, H6586

Webster Dictionary and Thesaurus. Nichols Publishing Group, 1999. 436, 722

26 Please note some aspects of repentance and forgiveness were adapted from material presented in:

Nancy Leigh DeMoss and Tim Grissom, *Seeking Him* (Life Action Ministries, 2004), 61-77, 169-189.

27 Lynette J. Hoy, *Safe Relationships, Women's 10-Weeks Series,* 2004. 5.

28 Please note aspects of conflict resolution were adapted from the following resources:

Lynette J. Hoy, *Safe Relationships, Women's 10-Weeks Series,*2004. 43-49.

Paul Hegdtrom, *Angry Men and the Women who Love Them.* (Beacon Hill Press, 1999, 2004), 102-104

29 Ed Wheat and Gloria Okes Perkins, *Love Life for Every Married Couple.* Grand Rapids, MI.: Zondervan, 1980. 31.

30   Paul Hegdtrom, *Angry Men and the Women who Love Them.* (Beacon Hill Press, 1999, 2004). 97-104.

31   Lynette J. Hoy, *Safe Relationships, Women's 10-Weeks Series*, 2004. 44-45.

32   Lynette J. Hoy, *Safe Relationships, Women's 10-Weeks Series*, 2004.

33   The Piggy Bank World Team, *The History of the Piggy Bank:* http://www.piggybank-world.com/History-of-the-Piggy-Bank-sp-65.html

34   Please note some of the information in the chapter titled, *The Piggy Bank* was adapted from: Association of Biblical Counselors, *Preparing a Budget*, 2006: www.christian-counseling.com

35   Webster's Dictionary and Thesaurus. Nichols Publishing Group, 1999. 322.

36   Jack Hayford, *study note*, Spirit Filled Life Bible, New King James Version, Thomas Nelson Inc., 1991.1424

37   James Strong, S.T.D.,LL.D., *Strong's Exhaustive Concordance of The Bible with Greek and Hebrew Dictionaries.* (Christian Hertiage Publishing Company, Inc., 1988). G1690, G4726, G2799, G1145, G4053, G2896. Webster's Dictionary and Thesaurus. Nichols Publishing Group, 1999. 365, 735. Webster's New World Thesaurus. Simon and Schuster, Inc., 1985. 806